MADE FOR THE OUTDOORS

LEN McDOUGALL

LYONS & BURFORD, PUBLISHERS

PRINTED IN THE UNITED STATES OF AMERICA

ILLUSTRATIONS © MANUEL F. CHEO FOR PAGES:III, 5, 53, 83, 99, 131, 153, 181
DESIGN BY KATHY KIKKERT

10 9 8 7 6 5 4 3 2 1

Library of Congress Cataloging-in-Publication Data
McDougall, Len.
     Made for the outdoors / Len McDougall.
          p.   cm.
     Includes index.
     ISBN 1-55821-329-5 (pbk.)
     1. Outdoor life—Equipment and supplies. I. Title.
GV191.6.M23   1995
796.5—dc20   95-8220
                                                         CIP

> THE PUBLISHER ASSUMES NO LIABILITY FOR THE USE OF THE
> MATERIALS OR METHODS DESCRIBED IN THIS BOOK, NOR FOR
> THE PRODUCTS THEREOF.

Gore Tex® is a registered trademark of W. L. Gore & Associates. Velcro® is a registered trademark of Velcro Industries. Thinsulate™ is a registered trademark of
3M Company.

To my loving wife Jacque,
whose patience, devotion, and faith
make anything possible.

CONTENTS

INTRODUCTION

O f all the things I've been or tried to be in my life, no one pursuit has held my interest as strongly as being a woodsman. For nearly three decades, my fascination with nature, survival, and woodcraft in general has never dimmed. I attribute that unwavering interest to the fact that woodsmanship is a school from which students can never graduate because total mastery of its vast array of subjects is simply unattainable. Every answered question only opens the door to a multitude of new questions, creating an ironic situation in which the more you learn, the dumber you feel. In my experience, learning to live with and within nature is the ultimate challenge.

But it's a fun and fulfilling challenge that can be enjoyed by almost everyone, young and old, rich and poor, male and female. Nature is the great equalizer; it strips away the false skin each of us is forced to wear in modern society, leaving only the basic human animal, and very often revealing things about us that we didn't know existed. We become part of an environment where social status is meaningless, where our worth is measured almost solely by our capacity for imagination and ingenuity.

Which brings us to the reason for this book. Over the years I've collected a wealth of ideas, projects, and techniques that have served to make life in the wilderness easier and more enjoyable. Many were taught to me by fellow woodsmen, many were adapted from existing technology, and a few might even be my own inventions, but all of them are the products of ingenuity fueled by necessity. The projects and methods described within these pages have all proved their worth many, many times, but I'd be a liar if I claimed that any of them were beyond further improvement.

I also think that the contents of this book are especially pertinent now that our species has begun in earnest to rectify at least some of the harm it's done to our planet's environment. The current trend toward recycling waste products is laudable, but it isn't a new idea by any means. Hikers, backpackers, and especially survivalists have definite limits on the number of items they can carry into the woods, which means that every piece of equipment must be as versatile as possible. Even something so basic as an empty soup can might be called upon to serve as a cooking vessel, drinking glass, rainwater reservoir, or bait container, while a simple length of fencing wire has so many uses in the woods that I couldn't begin to list them here. Our forebears practiced recycling by turning old boot soles into door hinges, saw blades into skinning knives, and glass bottles into candle holders. They would almost certainly have been horrified by modern society's cavalier disposal of something so potentially valuable as a plastic Tylenol bottle.

And, finally, the inevitable sales pitch, the reason I feel justified in asking you, the outdoorsman, to spend your hard-earned money on my book: Put simply, I think any hunter, angler, backpacker, or survivalist who buys this book will save enough money to cover his or her investment several times over. Many of the projects described in it are cheaply made (and sometimes improved) versions of commercially sold products. The replacement knife sheath project, for example, costs mere pennies, yet results in a sheath more durable and versatile than the majority of its mass-produced counterparts. Likewise, the baking technique given for weatherproofing leather boots works better and lasts far longer than even several applications of the high-priced boot greases, yet it uses plain old petroleum jelly. I'm willing to bet that everyone can find better uses for the money they will save by using these alternatives.

So take a hard look at the contents of this book before opening your wallet; you'll see that the book can withstand close scrutiny. If you decide that it wouldn't be a valuable addition to your outdoor gear, that's okay. But if you're an outdoorsman who enjoys meeting the challenges of the wilderness with ingenuity and creativity, I hope you'll be taking this copy home with you—because you're the person for whom I wrote it.

SECTION 1

CAMPING

FIRE WICK

MATERIALS NEEDED:

▼

Paraffin (canning wax)

▼

Cotton laundry string, 6'

▼

*Metal container,
for melting paraffin*

▼

Plastic 35mm film canisters

To the outdoorsman who really needs it, fire is the most important thing in the world. In the north country the difference between daytime and nighttime temperatures might be as much as 40 degrees Fahrenheit during even the summer months, and the warmth from a crackling campfire has many times meant the difference between spending an inconvenient but bearable night in the wilderness and suffering from a severe, even fatal case of hypothermia. Add to that the possibility of wet clothing from a rainstorm or accidental dunking, and you have a situation that can become very serious with the setting of the sun. The common truth in all of these cases is that if you can start and sustain a fire, you aren't going to freeze to death, no matter how cold the weather gets.

But one of nature's ironies is that a fire will typically become more necessary as the conditions for starting it become less favorable. Foresighted woodsmen tend to hedge their bets by using easily lighted materials that can produce enough heat to dry out and ignite wet natural tinder or twigs placed tepee-fashion above them. Modern fire-starting aids include chemical wonders like Trioxane, Hexamine, compressed "fire sticks," and the novel "fire ribbon," which resembles nothing so much as a tube of highly flammable toothpaste. All of these perform as advertised, but if you're the type of person who wants to get every penny's worth out of every dollar—and that describes most of us these days—then this project will probably be of interest to you.

The fire-starting aid I use most often is waterproof, effective, lightweight, and dirt cheap, or even free if you're a scavenger like myself. For lack of a better name, I call it the fire wick, because basically it's nothing more than an oversized candle wick without the candle.

I got the idea for the fire wick a few years ago, although I doubt very much that I was the first to discover something so simple. Like countless woodsmen before me, I always carried a candle in my gear to help start stubborn fires under wet conditions and to light and heat my shelter at night. The problem with ordinary candles was they had more wax than wick, which meant that I was always left with a blob of unused wax after the wick had been totally consumed. There had to be a more efficient method of balancing the amount of wick to the volume of wax needed to burn it completely.

As an experiment, I twisted up a four-foot length of double-thick candle wick from cotton laundry string, available from most arts and crafts stores. Wicks made from nylon string are difficult to light, burn poorly, and don't absorb paraffin well, so stick with cotton.

To increase the burn time of and heat generated by each wick, the string is doubled using the universal twist-lock method employed for making rope from plant fibers or multiplying the strength of any-diameter cordage. Begin the method by holding a length of string firmly in place at one end by whatever means is available (length permitting, I usually just stand

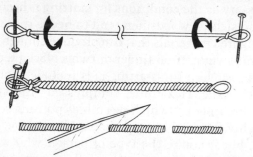

To make fire wicks, twist a length of cotton string as shown (top) until it has a tendency to coil around itself. Next, double the twisted string (center) and allow it to twist evenly to double thickness. Finally, immerse the twisted wick in melted paraffin, let it harden, and cut it into sections with a sharp knife (bottom).

on one end). Then twist the opposite, free end of the string in the same direction as the factory twist (usually clockwise), while keeping the string pulled taut. The number of turns required will vary with the length of the string, but twisting should continue until the string has a strong tendency to wind itself into coils when tension on it is eased.

But don't allow it to coil up just yet. Maintain a steady tension on the string and fold it in half, bringing the two ends together. The doubled end will immediately wind itself in a counterclockwise direction as the tension is slowly released. When the wick has coiled around itself evenly along its entire length, tie the loose ends together.

The next step is to dunk the finished wick in a container of melted paraffin. Melt the parrafin over an electric range or hot plate—never over an open flame, as paraffin is very flammable. When the wick is completely saturated with liquid wax, pull it from the vessel and stretch it taut while running it under a stream of cold water. An equally effective but slower method of cooling the wick is to simply hang it vertically for about fifteen minutes and let it air cool. Please remember at all times that melted paraffin is very flammable. It can also burn skin severely if touched, so be very careful.

After the wax has cooled to room temperature, the wick will be stiff enough to be laid across a cutting board and sliced into sections that fit inside a 35mm film canister. The nearly indestructible little film canisters, as well as screw-top pill bottles, are airtight, which makes them great for protecting small items like paper matches or ibuprofen tablets from moisture. But in this instance the canister is also a convenient place to carry the fire wicks. Saturated with paraffin, the wicks are completely impervious to water and can never become too wet to light.

Using the wicks is even easier than making them. In dry weather, remove the wick from its storage canister, and simply light one end as though it were a candle. Place it atop a bed of tinder, or even right on the ground. Next, build a low tepee of very small twigs over the flaming wick. When the tepee catches fire, add progressively larger sticks until the fire becomes a healthy, crackling blaze.

In wet or snowy weather, it works best to place the lighted wick on a small platform of sticks laid side-by-side on the ground and then place the tepee of twigs on top of that. Unlike Trioxane or Hexamine, which are difficult to extinguish once lighted, the wick can be put out by heavy rain, but if the burning wick is partially shielded by an umbrella of twigs it will start a fire in all but the most torrential of rainstorms. The wick can also be blown out by very high winds, although that will seldom be a problem because the wise woodsman always places a fire out of the wind to keep its heat as concentrated as possible and to prevent hot sparks from being blown all over the woods.

The average burn time of a single two-inch fire wick is just over two minutes, which is nearly always sufficient to get a fire going. In very wet conditions, the burn time and generated heat can both be increased by simply adding more wicks as necessary, but I've never needed to use more than three at one time. Of course, the drier the wood the better, and I recommend breaking off protruding dead twigs from fallen trees for your kindling rather than picking them up off the often-moist ground. Twigs and branches that are still attached to the trunks of fallen trees tend to shed water and dry quickly, while twigs on the ground have absorbed moisture.

A simpler—and some say better—alternative to using twisted cotton string is to saturate felt weather stripping with molten wax. Felt weather stripping is available in roll form at most hardware stores and it makes a very good substitute for cotton string. The procedure for making fire wicks from felt is exactly the same as it is for laundry string, except in this case the material is waxed as is and cut into sections. Felt fire wicks light easily if you fray the ends before applying flame, and they have a longer burn time due to their increased width, but felt is much more expensive than laundry string.

The fire wick hasn't replaced all my other fire-starting aids; the new Gerber Strike Force occupies a place of prominence in my survival harness and I still carry a bar of Trioxane in my ALICE (All-purpose Lightweight Individual Carrying Equipment) pack for those times when I need its tremendous heat to get a fire started quickly under the worst conditions. Even my hunting daypack contains a small folding Hexamine stove for whipping up hot meals without flame or smoke. But the low cost of cotton-string fire wicks allows hundreds of them to be made for just pennies, and that makes it possible to spread them throughout your gear, clothing, and vehicles so that at least several will always be on hand. After all, even the best fire-starting aid is useless if you don't have it with you; in that regard, its portability alone can make the fire wick better than the rest.

STARTING A FIRE, REGARDLESS

I awoke shivering. The first thought to register in my shocked mind was that the mountain tent in which I was sleeping had collapsed under a considerable amount of snow. Outside the mostly illusory protection of the nylon walls I could hear the howl of a driving northwest wind running through the hardwoods like a pack of spirit wolves on the hunt. It was 5:30 A.M. and I was very cold.

Fumbling in the predawn darkness, my half-numb fingers found the AM transistor radio in my knapsack and switched on WJML, in Petoskey, Michigan, the only local station in those days. I lay shivering in my inadequate sleeping bag as the irritatingly cheerful voice of the morning DJ informed listeners that an unpredicted cold front had blown in overnight with a foot of fresh snow and a temperature of –20 degrees, not counting wind chill. I was completely unprepared for that kind of weather, in terms of both equipment and experience.

I couldn't stay where I was, that much was obvious. Reluctantly, I crawled out of the meager warmth of my sleeping bag and pulled on my rock-hard insulated leather boots. After much wiggling and squirming, I managed to jam both feet into them, only to be rewarded with toes that went instantly numb with cold. My wool-lined leather gloves were also frozen stiff and I knew there would be no benefit from trying to shove unfeeling hands into them, so I pushed them into the waistband of my trousers to thaw.

When I crawled from the shambles of my mountain tent, the icy wind hit me full force and the skin over my cheekbones began to tingle almost immediately. The fire pit was completely covered with a white blanket and even though my fire had been banked well the night before, there wasn't a single coal left alive. The skin on my knuckles was already white from frostbite and my hands felt wooden as I struck nearly a dozen kitchen matches against a piece of paper birch bark. Between my violent shivering, the strong winds, and my unfeeling fingers, I couldn't get the bark to ignite. I burned one of my fingers severely striking the matches, but was too frozen to feel it until later.

That was in 1972. I was 16 and it was my first attempt at winter camping. I lived to learn from that experience only because I abandoned everything except my .410 shotgun and walked the six miles between camp and home. Had the circumstances been even slightly worse, my inability to start a fire and regain the precious body heat I'd lost would surely have meant my death. It was a painful lesson that I was lucky to learn.

I will never face that situation again, nor will anyone else who takes the time to put together an inexpensive, pocket-sized fire-starting kit and carries it along whenever he or she goes into the woods. It isn't enough to count on matches or a cigarette lighter alone because the times when a fire is most needed are almost invariably the times when it will be most difficult to get one started.

The trick to starting a fire in any weather is to select the instruments that will be most effective under the most inclement conditions. These will consist of an initial fire-starting tool—matches or a butane lighter, for instance—and flammable tinder that will produce an easily lighted, hot flame of sufficient duration to ignite wet or frozen wood.

Under most conditions, ordinary paper matches or wooden safety matches will be equal to the task, providing they're kept dry and used judiciously. But those who prefer to hedge their bets with matches that deliver optimum performance in any weather will find waterproof "lifeboat" matches a better choice. Lifeboat matches are distinguished from ordinary wooden matches by their oversized heads, which are approximately four times larger, and their waterproof varnish coatings. They will light under the wettest conditions, burn strongly for about twelve seconds, and stay lit even in a hard wind. The drawback is price; lifeboat matches are usually sold in five-packs of 25 matches per pack with an average retail price of about $10.00. That works out to roughly $.13 per match. You probably won't want to use them every time you start a fire.

The butane lighter is another wonder of technology that has lent itself well to the outdoorsman's needs. With a retail price of about $.80 and a thousand potential campfires in each lighter, it may be the most cost-effective fire-starting tool available. The only minor drawback is that the butane lighter won't light if it's been immersed in water, although if the striker wheel and flint are allowed to dry (or kept dry in the first place) it works as good as new until the gas is exhausted. Each component of my wilderness kit contains a butane lighter, the oldest of these being a decade-old Cricket that still lights. Even empty lighters can start fires (see "The Poor Man's Fire-Starting Kit," page 18).

But a set of matches or a lighter alone isn't adequate in a heavy rain or driving snow. The initial spark or flame must be complemented by a tinder material that ignites easily and quickly in wet, windy weather, burns hot, and stays lighted long enough to ignite wet twigs into a self-supporting flame. My personal favorite among these tinder materials is the US military Trioxane fuel tablet, originally designed to heat field rations without creating telltale smoke or flame. Trioxane tablets come individually packaged in resealable foil pouches, ignite with just the touch of a match, and stay lighted, regardless. They generally retail for about $2.00 for a box of three, but I've found that the price varies greatly from retailer to retailer, and the thrifty shopper can often find them for as little as $1.00 a box.

Another military combustible that has found favor with the civilian outdoorsman is the Hexamine fuel tablet sold by many outfitter stores and mail-order companies. The British army "Tommy Cooker" sold by Brigade Quartermasters of Kennesaw, Georgia, is a nifty little folding cookstove that uses Hexamine bars for fuel and sells for $7.00. Each of the fuel bars burns for 15 minutes and produces enough heat to boil a liter of water—or ignite wet twigs. Hexamine, while not quite as volatile or hot as Trioxane, lights easily, is unaffected by water or wind, and makes a very good tinder material for the fire-starting kit. Fuel bars for the Tommy Cooker are available separately and retail for $3.00 for a package of eight.

"Fire ribbon" is the newest of the chemical fire-starting agents to enter the outdoors market. The pasty substance comes packaged in a squeezable metal tube that allows it to be applied only as needed, and it too is unaffected by water. A tube of fire ribbon will start about thirty fires and retails for $3.00. The only problem I've seen with it is, the package so much resembles a tube of toothpaste that one of my companions nearly brushed his teeth with the stuff.

Fire wicks (see page 7), made from paraffin-saturated cotton string, have become an essential part of my own fire-starting kit. Basically just an oversized candle wick, the fire wick is waterproof, dirt cheap to make, and small enough to fit more than 100 into a shirt pocket.

The "Strike Force" fire-starting tool from Gerber Legendary Blades is one of many commercially manufactured fire-starting kits on the market, but at the time of this writing it's easily the best one ever made. The stout, pocket-sized unit snaps apart at the center to reveal a massive, half-inch-diameter flint rod mounted in one section and a high-carbon stainless steel striker mounted in the other. A snap-on cap in the butt of the flint half covers a storage compartment large enough to carry one Strike Force chemical tinder cube. But even without chemical tinder, the sparks generated by this tool—they actually become hotter with use—are sufficient to ignite dry pine needles and other tinder. The Strike Force retails for about $15.00 at outfitter stores and replacement tinder cubes sell for about $6.00 a dozen.

All the contrivances mentioned thus far provide just the initial step toward starting a fire; getting the most from each of them requires a bit of planning before the first match is struck. To begin with, a suitable location must be selected to combat the effects of wind and blowing snow or rain as much as possible. Natural terrain features such as gullies, hills, and thick woods are good windbreaks, so long as they're in a location where the fire can be easily contained. The fire should always be laid on the leeward side of a windbreak and, if at all possible, in an excavated pit with earth piled around its rim. Never lay the fire at the base of a tree because this presents a potential of burning, or at least killing, the upper branches, and many a winter woodsman (including myself) has had a hard-won fire extinguished by a clump of falling, half-melted snow.

In situations where there's too much snow on the ground to be scraped away, a platform will have to be laid atop the hard-pack to contain the burning tinder until the fire is strong enough to resist the effects of melting snow. The platform, made from a row of heavy branches placed adjacent to one another, will eventually burn and melt its way down to bare ground, but by the time it does, the fire will be too strong to be extinguished. A platform will also help in very wet or rainy weather.

The most common mistake made when attempting to build a fire in any weather is trying to build it too big too fast. After a suitable location has been selected and the tinder laid, the next step is to surround the unlighted tinder with a tepee of very small twigs, positioned so a small open-air space exists around each twig. This method makes the most efficient use of burning tinder by allowing each twig to dry and ignite independently. Bear in mind that wood doesn't actually burn; combustion is effected by heating the wood to its "flash point," the point at which it gives off combustible gases. Before that can happen, the water in it or on it must be driven out by evaporation. In very cold weather the combustion process will take a bit longer because any moisture contained in the wood will be frozen and must be thawed before it can be evaporated.

When starting a fire in wet weather or rain, dead twigs should be taken from fallen tree trunks rather than right off the ground because water will run off them rather than soak through and they'll be wet only on the outside. In a hard rain, it's also good practice to erect a second tepee over the first to form an umbrella that will protect the kindling below from being extinguished. By the time the lower tepee burns down to coals, the upper, larger tepee will be in flames and nothing short of a bucket of water will extinguish the fire.

For the sake of brevity, many fire-starting aids, some useful and some not worth carrying, have been ignored here. My only purpose is to provide information about putting together an effective fire-starting kit that will be easy to carry, inexpensive,

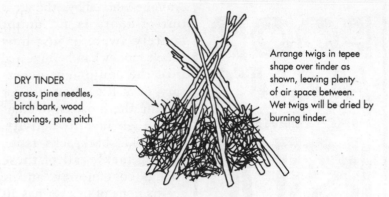

DRY TINDER
grass, pine needles,
birch bark, wood
shavings, pine pitch

Arrange twigs in tepee
shape over tinder as
shown, leaving plenty
of air space between.
Wet twigs will be dried by
burning tinder.

Starting a campfire—tepee method.

and capable of creating a warm, life-giving fire under the worst conditions nature can throw at a woodsman. The items recommended here will enable the most inexperienced to accomplish that goal.

The fire-starting kit may also be packaged to suit individual tastes, just so long as it remains convenient enough to ensure that it won't be left behind. My primary fire-starting kit is contained in an ordinary two-piece plastic soap dish, sold at most department and drug stores for about $1.00, and many of the newer survival-type knives sport external pouches that are roomy enough to pack in a second, smaller kit. I carry both, and every other component of my outdoor kit also includes some sort of fire-starting device.

In Canada and some of our own northern states, conditions cold enough to precipitate a dangerous case of hypothermia can arise without warning any month of the year, and not just when snow covers the ground. A cold rain in July can be just as dangerous to the backpacker or canoeist as a blizzard in November can be to the deer hunter, particularly since the summer outdoorsman is less apt to be equipped with cold-weather clothing. But regardless of how low the temperature drops or how poorly equipped the individual may be, the ability to build and sustain a fire will always prevent an uncomfortable situation from becoming worse.

POOR MAN'S FIRE-STARTING KIT

MATERIALS NEEDED:

▼

Mini-Bic butane lighter, empty

▼

Twist- or snap-cap pill bottle

▼

Cotton batting from pill bottle

▼

Fire wicks

Anyone who enjoys the great out-of-doors is no doubt acutely aware of just how much money can be invested into the equipment necessary, or at least desirable, for getting the most enjoyment from their favorite activity. Guns, skis, backpacks, tents, fishing tackle; all of these things cost money, and it seems none of us ever has all the gear we think we need. But our enjoyment of the outdoors shouldn't be limited by the thickness of our wallets, so it always gives me pleasure to pass along any discoveries that might help fellow outdoor enthusiasts save money. Very few of us have money to burn these days and every dollar saved on equipment is a dollar that can be spent on something else. The fire-starting kit described here makes use of materials that are normally considered useless. In fact all three of the components used to make it are recycled.

The kit begins with a disposable butane lighter from which all the gas has been exhausted. Any empty flint-type lighter will work (piezo-electric lighters will not), but I prefer to use minisized Bics because they take up less space. As probably most of us know, the flint in these lighters always outlasts the butane supply, so even though the stored gas may be gone, the lighter will still produce hundreds of sparks. And where a spark exists, there exists the potential for fire—with the right tinder.

Turning an empty butane lighter into an effective sparking device is a simple operation. Just remove the metal flame hood

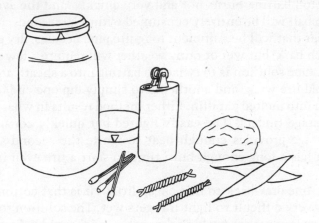

A very effective fire-starting kit can be made by placing an empty Mini-Bic butane lighter, cotton, fire wicks, and matches inside an empty, watertight pill bottle.

by bending it out at either side with a pair of needle-nosed pliers. The brass gas valve at the front of the lighter and the thumb lever that activates it can be left where they are. Neither the valve nor the lever will hinder the lighter's ability to throw a spark, and removing either requires that the striker wheel, flint, and flint compression spring be removed first. Disassembly is simple, but reassembly of the striker entails compressing the flint and spring while inserting the striker wheel, and that can be infuriatingly tricky.

Since lighters are designed to ignite butane or naphtha gases, both of which are extremely flammable, the spark produced is small. That means the tinder used in this kit has to be not only common and easily transportable, but very flammable. Cotton batting, found in every bottle of aspirin or vitamins, is ideal, as are cotton balls and cotton makeup pads.

To ignite the cotton, first fray one edge until the individual fibers are loose and airy. Hold this loosened mass as close to the lighter's exposed thumbwheel as possible and strike a spark into it. If a breeze is blowing, it may be necessary to shield the tinder from it with your body. After no more than three attempts, the tinder should be in flames.

Cotton batting burns hot and very quickly, and the average cotton ball will be entirely consumed within 10 seconds. In dry weather that will be sufficient to ignite pine needles, dry grass, or birch bark, but wet or rainy weather will require a few more BTUs. One solution is to twist the batting into a sheath around a waxed fire wick, and another is to simply dip one end of the cotton into melted paraffin. Either method results in what I call "two-stage tinder." The easily lighted but quickly consumed first stage provides enough heat to ignite the second stage, which has a long enough burn time to start a fire even in the rain.

The one drawback to this cheap little kit is that cotton batting is very difficult to light if it gets wet. The solution to that problem is as easy as packing the cotton, wicks, and lighter into the same bottle the cotton came in. Many types of waterproof pill bottles with either screw or snap caps are large enough to hold a small butane lighter and enough tinder to light a dozen fires. Some also have childproof caps, which is probably best if you have small children who might find the kit's workings fascinating. To make the kit even more effective in foul weather, the cotton wicks can be complemented with one of Gerber's biodegradable Strike Force tinder cubes, which are waterproof, windproof to 35 MPH, and can be lighted directly from the lighter's spark.

There's really no reason why this practically cost-free kit wouldn't serve well as a woodsman's primary fire-starting tool, or in the thinking man's survival kit. But even if you've already spent your money on a commercial firestarter, the poor man's fire-starting kit can come in handy for friends, as a back-up, or just for making sure that every vehicle, hunting blind, or fish shanty is equipped to get a fire going. Why not? The price is certainly right.

BUDDY BURNER

This section describes how to make and use one of the best portable camp stoves I've found yet. It's called a Buddy Burner and I learned about it many years ago from my kid brother, who was a Cub Scout at the time. This little stove is so portable and efficient—not to mention downright cheap— that it's hard to believe someone isn't manufacturing it commercially.

The Buddy Burner is essentially nothing more than a large candle in a can with a metal lid. What gives it the heat needed to boil water and cook food is its large wick, which can be half an inch in diameter or even larger. The oversized wick produces a hotter flame and absorbs well enough to keep it from "drowning" in molten wax the way smaller-wicked candles are prone to do.

Making the Buddy Burner is a simple procedure. All you need are a clean metal paint or Sterno can with a metal lid, a package of paraffin, and about six feet of cotton laundry string. The size of can you use will depend on how portable you want your stove to be. I have made very large Buddy Burners from two-pound coffee cans or gallon paint cans for heating shelters, warming frozen engines to get them started, and even keeping water pipes from freezing during long, cold, northern Michigan winters, but these are too large for a backpack or survival kit. The best choices for field-type Buddy Burners are small paint cans or the less sturdy aluminum Sterno cans because their metal lids make extinguishing the little stoves safe and easy.

The first step in putting together a Buddy Burner is making the wick. This procedure is exactly the same as the one used to make fire wicks (see pages 8–11), except in this case the wick is twisted and doubled three times to obtain a thickness of eight strands. Again, cotton string is the only kind that should be used to make the wick. A good alternative to making your own wick is to use one or two lengths of cotton kerosene lamp wicking or felt weather stripping. In either case, the wick you use should be saturated with hot wax and allowed to cool prior to using it.

Next, cut the blocks of paraffin into small pieces on a cutting board and fill the can with them. When the can will accept no more wax, set it in a heavy skillet or pan and place both on a hot plate or electric kitchen range set to no higher than medium heat. As the wax melts, its volume in the can will decrease, and more pieces can be added until the molten paraffin is no less than half an inch from the top of the can. Bear in mind that melted paraffin is flammable and that a momentary lapse of concentration could result in very severe burns.

When all the wax has melted, remove the pan and can from the heat. Measure how much wick is needed to reach the bottom of the can by holding it against the side of the can and running a piece of stiff wire (wire coat hangers work well) through the wick where it reaches the can's rim. The wire will be used to bridge the can's opening and hold the wick in place until the paraffin solidifies. Insert the wick into the molten wax and position it at the center of the can opening using the wire bridge.

At room temperature the wax in your new Buddy Burner will take about two hours to completely harden. Cooling time

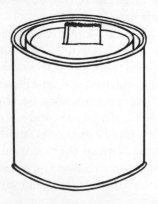

The Buddy Burner is essentially a large candle with an oversized wick inside a metal paint or Sterno can. It works very well as a camp stove, emergency heater, or lamp, and the metal lid makes extinguishing it a snap.

can be reduced by adding cold water and ice cubes to the pan in which it sits, or by just putting it in the refrigerator. After cooling, remove the wire, use a sharp knife to trim the wick, and snap on the lid. The Buddy Burner is ready for use.

When using the Buddy Burner as a heater or for light, simply pry off the top and light its wick as though it were an ordinary candle. To use it as a cookstove, excavate a trench in the soil wide enough to accommodate the can and about four inches deeper than the can is tall. Set the Buddy Burner in the bottom of the trench, light the wick, and place your cooking vessel across the trench directly over the flame. The sides of the trench will act as ventilation tunnels to keep the flame burning hot, while the earth above it provides a steady base for the cooking vessel.

The Buddy Burner will bring a quart of water to a rolling boil in under 15 minutes and will heat a can of soup in less time than that. Its barely visible, smokeless flame makes it an ideal choice for deer hunters who want to enjoy a warm meal and a hot cup of coffee during their long wait for the venison to show up.

Extinguishing the Buddy Burner is as easy as setting the metal lid into place over the can opening. Don't press it down completely until the wax cools, as the heat inside might cause it to pop off with enough force to send it sailing. The flame can also be blown out by a quick, forceful puff, but remember that the wax inside will be in its liquid state, so exercise caution. After cooling, the lid can be pressed firmly in place and the stove packed away for later use.

Burn time for a pint-sized Buddy Burner is three to four hours, depending on how large the wick is, and after the supply of wax has been exhausted the burner can be refilled. That makes the vessel of the Buddy Burner completely recyclable and in keeping with our current, environmentally enlightened trends.

So don't throw away those empty paint or Sterno cans; turn them into Buddy Burners. Few camp stoves can outdo the Buddy Burner in terms of price, portability, and performance, so you might want to make several and keep them on hand.

CANDLE LANTERN

A savvy old man once told me, "Never buy anything you can make yourself. You'll save money and maybe even end up with a better product." The years have impressed upon me the wisdom contained in that old-timer's words and I never fail to apply his advice whenever possible. Some of the most functional pieces of outdoor equipment I own have been handmade or adapted from an existing product to meet specific needs. There's a nice feeling of satisfaction that goes with being able to rely on an outdoor item you've made with your own hands, and it's always fun to exercise your creative abilities to duplicate or even improve upon the factory model.

One of the most utilitarian yet easily constructed of the many hunting, camping, or fishing items that can be made at home is the candle lantern. Using a candle to provide light is nothing new; throughout history people like Christopher Columbus, Florence Nightingale, and Abraham Lincoln have worked and read in the subdued light cast by a flickering taper, and today there are even a few manufactured lanterns that use the paraffin candle as a source of illumination. A single dinner-sized taper can throw enough light to read by, allow safe passage through rooms during a power outage, and even work as an emergency automotive trouble light.

Aside from its open flame, which is always potentially hazardous in the out-of-doors, the biggest drawback to using a candle for lighting is that it can be blown out by mild breezes. Both of these problems can be remedied by putting the lighted candle in an ordinary glass jar with a ventilated metal screw-on lid.

The flame is then contained and protected from the wind while the clear glass walls of the jar allow emitted light to radiate in all directions.

Just about any type of normally discarded jar will work to make a candle lantern, although canning and mayonnaise-type jars are probably the easiest to work with because of their large mouths and straight walls. The first step is to install a metal cup in the bottom of the jar to hold the melted wax and keep the glass bottom from becoming too hot to handle. The wax reservoir can be a tuna fish or cat food can if the jar mouth is large enough, but a metal jar lid placed upside down on the jar floor works best. Smaller lanterns can be fueled by tea candles, which are already contained in their own metal cups. The wax reservoir is held in place at the center of the jar bottom by applying a blob of hot glue, RTV adhesive, or a similar glue to its underside and sticking it in place.

The next step is to insert the candle. Any type of candle can be made to work, but large-diameter votive candles are my first choice. A single votive candle will provide useful light—and heat—for about eight hours, yet cost about a quarter of what you'd pay for "emergency" candles. Whichever type of candle you use, you should light it and allow it to burn until a small pool of melted wax forms at the base. When the wax cools it will adhere to the metal bottom of the reservoir and hold the candle firmly in place.

The metal screw-on lid can be an important component of the candle lantern because it helps to protect the burning candle from being extinguished by a stiff wind and provides a secure place from which to hang the lantern. If the lid has a cardboard gasket, it must be removed. If the lid has a plastic coating, try to remove it first. Or you can burn it off the first time the lantern is used. With a knife or screwdriver, punch as many holes in the lid as it will hold. Many small holes work better than a few large ones because they break up the wind better while still allowing enough air inside to keep the flame alive. If a knife is used to pierce the lid, twisting the blade will widen the holes into a triangle shape that provides better ventilation than a simple slit.

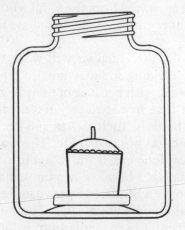

Most any clear jar can be made into an effective lamp by gluing an inverted metal jar cap to the bottom and placing a candle inside it. A votive candle (shown) burns for about eight hours and the jar protects its flame from being blown out.

The final step is to fit a snap-closed (notebook) binder ring through two of the holes in the center of the lid. Closed and locked in place, the binder ring is a convenient way to hang the lantern from an overhead tree branch to maximize the amount of space illuminated by it. But keep in mind that a significant amount of heat will be radiated through the lid and the binder ring will become very hot. Always use wire or a length of light chain with a clip on the end to suspend the lantern overhead, leaving about two feet between the lantern and the branch from which it's suspended.

Or you might opt to leave the jar lid off altogether if the jar is tall enough to negate the effect of wind on the candle's flame. In this case, the lamp can be suspended from a wire loop placed around the jar mouth and twisted up snugly on either side to leave two smaller loops on opposite sides of the mouth. The molded threads on the jar's neck will prevent the wire from sliding off, and the two loops will provide a convenient way to hang the lamp.

The candle lantern is a functional tool that seems especially appropriate for our changing times and attitudes. It utilizes items that have little value to anyone but a recycling company to make a piece of equipment that will certainly prove to be very handy around the camp, and perhaps invaluable during a power outage at home or on a long stretch of deserted highway at night. In cold weather the heat produced by the candle lantern can be used to warm a chilled deer-hunter's hands. It can provide enough light to read a book. (However, *never* bring any kind of flame into a tent or potentially flammable shelter). I know one man who uses the candle lantern to keep the oil pan of his car warm on subzero winter nights (don't laugh, his car always starts in the morning). I only wish that all of my outdoor gear were as inexpensive and useful as the candle lantern.

HOT BED

MATERIALS NEEDED:

▼

*A good, strong fire
(with lots of coals)*

▼

Folding shovel (optional)

▼

"Workable" soil

During a recent winter backpacking trip, one of my companions asked how I would manage to stay warm overnight if I didn't have a good sleeping bag. Questions like that are common and even predictable, so I was prepared with a ready answer. Rather than offer a simple verbal explanation, I decided it would be best to allow him to experience one solution to that dilemma for himself. It was mid-January and the outside temperature was a windless −10 degrees, perfect for proving (or disproving) the effectiveness of cold-weather survival techniques and equipment.

The technique I chose to demonstrate is called the "hot bed," or "coal bed." The hot bed isn't a new development, but a very old and valuable cold-weather survival tool that was largely forgotten during our headlong rush into the shackles of civilization. The movie *Jeremiah Johnson* briefly depicted the hot bed in a scene in which "Bearclaw" Chris Lapp, played by the late Will Geer, showed tenderfoot Robert Redford how to survive a winter night in the Rocky Mountains. Beyond that, it's tough to find references to the hot bed anywhere, which is unfortunate.

As with most of the best survival techniques, the principle behind the hot bed is simple: a red-hot bed of coals is covered with an insulating layer of loose soil that indirectly radiates steady warmth into the sleeper's body throughout the night. Lacking air, the coals will of course die out eventually, but my own experience has shown that the heat generated by a hot bed will continue for about ten hours, more than adequate to ensure a good night's rest.

Since the hot bed is most likely to be needed in subfreezing temperatures, let's begin by assuming that the ground is frozen and covered by several inches of snow. The first step is to build a large, hot fire to melt the surrounding snow, thaw the earth below, and provide a heat source of glowing coals. Once the fire is burning strongly, spread it over an area about three feet wide by seven feet in length and keep this extended fire burning for about thirty minutes. Then scrape the coals to one side, leaving an area of thawed earth large enough to accommodate a human body in repose. A slab of wood pulled from the outside of a rotting stump or log works well enough for scraping hot coals, but a folding shovel or entrenching tool makes the whole operation a lot easier from start to finish.

The next step is to excavate a shallow, body-sized trench at least six inches deep in the thawed soil. There will certainly be a number of tree and shrub roots to chop through so you can best accomplish this task with a quality folding shovel, although a machete, a hatchet, or even a survival knife will work well enough to do the job. As you loosen the soil, remove it and pile it to one side because you will reuse it later.

When the trench is complete, shovel or scrape the hot coals into its bottom. If the coals have cooled, or if there aren't enough to cover the bottom of the trench to a depth of about three inches, you can complement them with fresh coals from the campfire. If that isn't feasible, the simplest solution is to rebuild a fire in the bottom of the trench, which will reheat the existing charcoal and create an additional layer of fresh red coals.

The final step is to cover over the hot bed with the dirt taken from the trench during its excavation. *For safety's sake, there should **never** be less than four inches of loose soil laid atop the coals.* Throwing a ground sheet, such as a poncho or shelter half, over the covering soil will help to hold it in place as you roll in your sleep. If a ground sheet isn't available, a thin layer of green pine or cedar boughs will help to contain the loose soil. Be sure, though, to cover *all* coals for safety's sake. Finally, be absolutely sure to fully extinguish all coals once you are done with the hot bed by saturating the area with water.

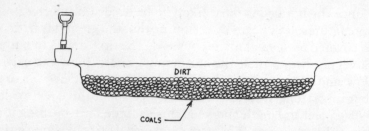

The hot bed is a very old device once used by Native Americans and fron-tiersmen whose bedrolls provided inadequate warmth during cold nights. It supplies a constant warmth for up to 10 hours, allowing campers to get a restful night's sleep.

An alternate method that can be used only when the ground is unfrozen is to first lay or create a bed of coals directly atop the ground, and then cover it with dirt taken from elsewhere. This method requires a bit less effort, but only if the ground is above freezing. Be especially careful with loose coals in this scenario. I personally prefer the trench type of hot bed because the hot coals are better contained and there is far less chance that you will burn either yourself or your equipment as you change positions throughout the night.

Under the worst conditions (i.e., frozen ground, snow, and little equipment), creation of a hot bed from start to finish will take two to three hours. But those are the same conditions in which a lost or injured deer hunter might be forced to lay up for a day or so, and once the initial effort has been made, the hot bed can be used over and over with little additional work. After the coals have died, the loose soil covering them can be scraped away with only gloved hands and the coals replenished to provide another night of warmth. The process can be repeated indefinitely, until the spring thaw if necessary.

The hot bed can also be employed—*carefully*—inside an in-flammable, emergency shelter. Laid inside a well-built makeshift shelter (for example, one made of green limbs or boughs which will not burn, or an igloo or snowcave) that has been sealed against wind and snow, the hot bed will not only keep a sleeping person warm all night but will actually serve to raise the temperature inside the shelter to a comfortable level.

Again, be sure to cover *all* coals with adequate topsoil.

As cold-weather survival procedures go, the hot bed is one of the best because it allows the outdoorsman with just a knife, a fire-starting kit, and the clothes on his or her back to sleep in relative comfort through the coldest night. One old-timer who used to live the more or less enviable life of a railroad hobo claims that he once survived a bitterly cold Wyoming night by constructing a hot bed and covering himself with loose dirt up to his neck.

The hot bed is far too valuable to allow it to become lost in history. Just make sure you put enough dirt down before going to sleep.

COFFEEBAGS

MATERIALS NEEDED:

▼

1 old sock or T-shirt, laundered

▼

Needle and thread

▼

1 shoelace

When a large coffee company recently began producing its innovative new single-serving coffeebags, some of my more experienced swamp-tromping brethren met the news with raised eyebrows and feigned astonishment. Their surprise was real, however, when they took note of the price tag affixed to this latest supermarket item.

Long-range backpackers and trophy hunters who find it necessary to venture deep into wilderness areas enjoy their coffee like anyone else, but can seldom justify the bulk and noise of a percolator pot in their packs when conditions demand traveling as lightly and quietly as possible. They usually settle for instant coffee, tea, or the more expensive manufactured coffeebags. Of course, any source of caffeine is better than none at all, but a hot, freshly brewed cup of ground coffee goes a long way toward eliminating early morning growls around the camp.

Putting ground coffee in a flow-through package so it can be swished around in hot water and the results swallowed down without choking on grounds is not a new concept; "swampers"

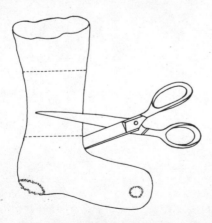

Most any sock will have an intact ankle section long after the toes and heels have worn through, which can be cut off and made into a coffeebag, or other useful items.

like myself have been using it to stave off the effects of caffeine withdrawal for years. Nor is it one that's beyond the means of even the most modest budget. Freshly brewed coffee is a luxury that all of us can enjoy without loading a bulky coffeepot into the backpack or taking on a second job.

The best material I've found for making coffeebags is from the ankle portion of an old sock, the one part that never seems to wear out. Cutting a six-inch section from this cloth tube with scissors is the first step. Next, turn the tube inside out and sew one end securely closed, bearing in mind that the stitches must be tight and close or you'll end up spitting grounds. With that completed, turn the tube, which is now a bag, right side out and sew a rolled hem around the opening to keep it from unraveling. Finally, sew an eight-inch piece of shoelace or heavy string to the outside of the bag, about an inch below the hem. A cotton T-shirt can also be used, although it will lack the elastic feature of a sock.

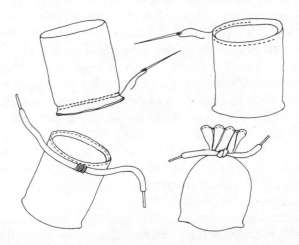

There are four steps involved in making a coffeebag: (1) sew together the bottom of the ankle tube from a discarded sock, forming a bag; (2) sew a hem around the bag's mouth; (3) sew a length of shoelace or similar cord to the bag's outside, below its mouth; (4) add the desired amount of coffee, tea, or herbs, tie the bag shut, and toss it into a container of boiling water.

To use the finished coffeebag, just spoon in the desired amount of grounds, tie the bag tightly shut by wrapping the shoelace around it several times and tying it off with a square knot, and drop the sealed package into a container of boiling water. If you think that sounds like even less fuss than making coffee at home, you're right.

Any type of coffee works well with this method, but the finely ground automatic drip coffee will make more brew for the money and help to stretch the woodsman's dollar. The measure of coffee grounds used will of course depend on individual tastes, but my rule of thumb is generally one teaspoonful of coffee per eight-ounce cup. Whatever your desired potency, a steady boil of five minutes is sufficient to brew as much flavor as possible out of the grounds.

The real beauty of this method is that it reuses everything except the grounds. Spent coffee grounds, which some flower gardeners use as fertilizer, can be shaken out directly onto the forest floor. The cloth pouch needs only a light rinsing in fresh water to make it ready for another brewing, and a single coffeebag will make dozens of pots of coffee before showing any signs of wear.

As for which type of material works best and whether or not colored material is safe to use—the two questions most asked about this project—it doesn't seem to make any difference. By the time a sock becomes a candidate for this project, it will have been laundered dozens of times and any remaining dyes will be fixed in the material. The only requirement as far as type of material is concerned is that it be a dense enough weave to contain the grounds. After many years of drinking coffee made from many types and colors of coffeebags, I've never experienced any ill effects or tasted anything but good coffee. Nor has any of my companions.

Aside from a substantial cost savings over manufactured single-serving coffeebags, the cloth coffeebag provides the flexibility to make brewed coffee in any desired amount, from a cup to a gallon, simply by varying the amount of grounds used. Even better, it takes up almost no room at all, so you can carry as many spares as you have old socks. And best of all, these coffeebags are made from material that would probably otherwise end up in the trash.

SPICE-BOTTLE SALT AND PEPPER SHAKERS

It has always amazed me that a market even exists for "campers'" salt and pepper shakers. The market does exist, however, and the fact that they continue to be marketed year after year is a pretty good indication that someone is buying salt and pepper shakers specifically made (or at least marketed) for outdoorsmen.

The irony of this situation is that campers and backpackers are funding the manufacture of new shaker bottles, while at the same time throwing away (hopefully to the recycling bin) millions of empty spice bottles that will work at least as well as those sold by camping supply outlets. Probably everyone who uses a kitchen has a cupboard stocked with seasoned salt, garlic powder, and other commercially packaged spices, most of them contained in rugged plastic shaker bottles. I often use a packaged spice as is to enhance the flavor of campfire cooking, but when the bottle is empty, I simply refill it with salt or pepper, the woodsman's two most important spices.

Some of the newer spice bottles are being fitted with screw-on caps that have shaker holes molded into them. When not in use, the holes are closed by a flip-up cover to prevent spills. These will work for camping, but I don't recommend them for the backpack because they tend to open without warning and dump all over. The best candidates are three-piece types, con-

BLACK PEPPER

It's silly to spend money on "campers'" salt and pepper shakers when there's a ready supply of free—and larger—shaker bottles with screw-down caps in the kitchen cupboard.

sisting of the bottle and a screw-on cap with a separate snap-on shaker cap. To refill these bottles, remove the top and pry the shaker cap from the bottle mouth with a thumbnail. Fill the bottle with salt, pepper, or another spice and replace the caps. I also recommend removing the factory label and relabeling the bottle with the correct contents, especially if you're a campfire gourmet who carries several kinds of spices.

Nor are these handy little bottles limited to just holding spices. I carried one of the large bottles filled with instant coffee for six years before it finally melted because someone (okay, it was me) left it sitting too close to the campfire. These watertight, practically indestructible containers can also be used to carry a two-day supply of rice, oatmeal, or other dried foodstuffs, as fire-starting or sewing kits, or even as pocket-sized tackleboxes for lures. As with most everything else, the uses a woodsman can find for them is limited only by his or her ingenuity.

SOAPBAG

MATERIALS NEEDED:

▼

1 old wool sock

▼

Needle and thread

▼

1 shoelace

▼

Bar soap

One of my favorite reasons for backpacking into the wilderness is to escape the silly social restrictions of "civilized" life, where people are judged by the labels on their clothing, the kind of car they drive, and how well they conform to a multitude of other more or less meaningless social standards. In the woods, what really matter are things like a good knife and a comfortable pair of boots, while things like underarm odor or un-minty breath become just what they are, normal functions of the human body.

But after two or three days, everyone wants—and needs—a bath. Smelling nice doesn't mean much in the woods, but cleanliness is still needed to prevent infecting minor wounds and to avoid skin eruptions caused by clogged pores. The problem is that wet bar soap is messy, is hard to hang onto, and attracts a variety of undesirable debris, from hairs and gnats to tree bark and gravel. Lathering up with a bar of soap after it's fallen into sand is like scrubbing with sandpaper.

The soapbag solves all these problems: its wrist loop allows the soap to be suspended securely while leaving the hands free; foreign particles wash off easily; and the soap can be hung to dry when the bath is finished. Washing with the soap contained inside a cloth pouch guarantees that every bit of it will be used up, while the pouch around it functions very well as a washcloth.

To start with, I like to use an old wool sock whose toes and heels have been worn beyond repair. I prefer to use wool because its mildly abrasive texture is great for scrubbing off the dust and sweat accumulated from several days on the trail, but folks with sensitive skin can use cotton, nylon, or another smooth material. Cut the ankle portion off the bottom of the sock and then cut another eight-inch section from that. In most

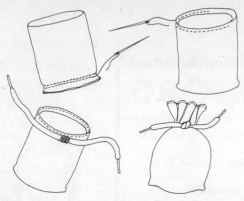

By cutting the ankle tube from a worn-out wool sock, sewing it into a tie-closed bag as shown, and dropping in a bar of soap, campers can have an easily gripped, dirt-free combination soap and washcloth for scrubbing off trail dust.

cases, the long ankle tube of a hunting or hiking sock will yield at least two soapbags.

Next, turn the section of ankle tube inside out and roll over one end, around the outside, to form a half-inch hem. With a needle and ordinary thread, fasten the rolled hem to the tube under it with a wide, long, "basting" stitch around the tube's perimeter. Then, press the sides of the hemmed end together and sew the bottom closed with a row of short, snug stitches running from one end to the other and back again. Another hem around the open end of the bag will help to keep it from becoming frayed and result in a prettier finished product, but it really isn't necessary.

After the hems and bottom of the bag have been securely stitched, turn the bag right side out. The final step is to sew a shoelace (other types of light cord will also work) to the side of the open end, about half an inch below the mouth. These stitches should be applied at the center of the cord and need run only a quarter inch or so of its length, just enough to ensure that the cord and bag are securely attached together.

To ready the soapbag for use, simply fill it with a bar of soap and tie the end closed by wrapping the cord tightly around its mouth two full turns and tying it off with a square knot. Another square knot at the ends of the cord forms a wrist loop that will prevent the soapbag from being dropped and washed away by swift currents or lost in deep water.

One of the nicer features of the soapbag is that it completely uses every bit of soap placed inside it, which makes it a good solution to the problem of all those mostly used scraps of bar soap that always seem to accumulate in the bathroom. In fact, I like the soapbag so much I have one hanging in my shower at home, while my wife swears by it for washing countertops and loosening tough stains in clothing.

But the place where the soapbag really shines is in the woods. Incorporating soap and a washcloth in one package makes it easy to handle and allows the soap to be air dried before restowing it in the pack. As further protection against contaminating other equipment and clothing with scented soap residue, the unit fits neatly into a hinged plastic soap dish, available from most drug and department stores. Hey, everyone enjoys getting a little grubby on camping trips, but the soapbag makes getting clean a lot easier and more convenient once the novelty of being dirty starts wearing thin.

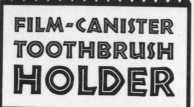

FILM-CANISTER TOOTHBRUSH HOLDER

MATERIALS NEEDED:

▼

35mm plastic film canister (empty) and cap

▼

Shoelace or cord, 4"

No area of personal hygiene should have more importance to the woodsman than proper dental care. I would no more leave my toothbrushes (I carry at least two) behind on a camping trip than I would my compass or knife. Fresh minty breath is a nice option, but even without toothpaste, a good brushing morning and night will go a long way toward preventing toothaches, gum infections, and potentially dangerous abscesses that could bring on a raging fever overnight. Suffering from a painful toothache will also weaken your concentration, dull your senses, and make thinking clearly a real chore, which can lead to errors in judgment. Smelly armpits and dirty clothing aren't likely to do anything worse than keep your companions upwind, but an unclean mouth could spell genuine health problems in the backwoods.

As with any vital pieces of gear, it pays to treat your toothbrushes with care to maximize their useful life. An uncased toothbrush is likely to attract insects with its sweet residual odor of toothpaste, and it will certainly collect dirt, plant debris, and any number of other foreign materials that could make you hesitate to put it back in your mouth. Besides all that, it just feels better to know that such a personal tool of hygiene is securely encased.

The best toothbrush holder I've found for both the backpack and the bathroom at home is made from a common 35mm plastic film canister—just one of many uses for these useful little containers. Begin by very carefully cutting a small oval in the center of the cap with a razor knife or a very sharp penknife, just large enough to allow the toothbrush handle to slide through. This operation is most easily performed by laying the cap, top side down, on a cutting board where it can be held stable while cutting. To achieve the snuggest fit possible between the toothbrush handle and the hole in the cap, start with an undersized hole and then enlarge it a sliver at a time, using the toothbrush handle as a gauge. A very tight fit will probably not be possible due to the shape of most toothbrush handles, but that's okay because some ventilation is needed to let moisture evaporate between brushings and prevent mildew. The important thing is that the bristles be well protected.

Next, very carefully drill an eighth-inch hole in the cap, independent of the handle slot and as close to the molded snap-down ring as possible. A second hole is then drilled through the canister itself, about a half inch below the rim. Don't use the knife tip to drill these holes because the possibility of a slip is too great. Instead, use a section of coat hanger wire, a small punch, or a similar tool heated over a candle flame to melt through the plastic. A woodburner or soldering iron will also work, providing the tip is small enough.

The purpose behind these holes is to allow the cap and canister to be attached to one another with a four-inch length of shoelace or similar cord. Shove one end of the string through the hole in the canister from its outside, pull it through, and tie a single knot in the end to keep it from pulling back out. Then push the free end of the cord through the hole in the top of the cap and tie it off the same way. When you've finished, both knots will be inside the capped canister and its two components will be inseparable. All that remains is to insert your toothbrush handle through the slotted hole in the cap and snap the cap in place over the canister's mouth.

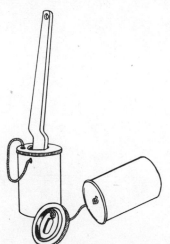

With nothing more than a 35mm film canister, a piece of string, and a sharp knife, outdoorsmen can make a toothbrush holder that outperforms its manufactured counterparts in the field and at home, while at the same time recycling items that might otherwise be discarded.

The type of film canister and cap used to make this tooth-brush holder isn't critical, but for camping I prefer to use one made from clear plastic, especially in warm weather. Hanging the encased toothbrush from a convenient tree branch by the cord, which forms a convenient loop when the canister is closed, will keep it free of dirt while drying and clear plastic will allow mildew-killing sunlight to penetrate within.

A toothbrush is easily the single most forgotten piece of equipment among outdoorsmen of all disciplines. The film-canister toothbrush holder can help to remedy that problem by making it convenient to include a cased toothbrush in every backpack or survival kit. And unlike some of the factory-made toothbrush holders I've tried, this one will serve its owner well for many years. There are no plastic hinges to break and both components are securely connected to one another. Best of all, it puts to good use a waste item that film developers toss into the recycling bin by the thousands. The only drawback is to the manufacturers of toothbrush holders, because you might never purchase one of their products again.

CAMPER'S SUNKEN BATHTUB

MATERIALS NEEDED:

▼

1 large sheet clear, heavy-mil plastic, approx. 8' × 8'

▼

1 backpacking (trowel) shovel (optional)

▼

Canteens/cooking pots (anything for transporting water)

Although this project might sound as though it belongs in a posh condominium, the sunken bathtub described here is actually a very practical luxury for the *long-term* camper and backpacker. While the day hiker or weekend camper will have minimal bathing requirements, most of us eventually crave a hot bath after four or five days in the backcountry. A sun-warmed inland lake is ideal for a quick "dip," but in many places the only source of water is frigid, spring-fed streams. I've bathed in a good many of these and it has never been a pleasant experience.

The sunken bathtub provides a much nicer alternative for the long-term camper or backpacker. In my first book, *Practical Outdoor Survival*, I recommended carrying a large eight-foot by eight-foot sheet of clear, heavy-mil plastic because it has so many possible uses in the wilderness, from waterproofing a shelter to distilling water to collecting rain. It also makes a dandy field-expedient bathtub (in lieu of plastic, a foil-laminated space blanket will work equally well).

The first step is to look around carefully for a depression in the ground, preferably in a sunny location. [To comply with sound environmental practices, keep your bathtub **at least 100 feet** from any natural water source. And be sure to check with park rangers and park publications for each park's specific water-use guidelines, and make sure your tub (if permitted) complies with those guidelines.] The depression should be about a foot deep by three feet wide by four feet long, or large enough to accommodate your body in a sitting position. Most any hole in the ground can be made to work if its initial dimensions are adequate. Remove any sticks, rocks, or other sharp protrusions that might puncture the plastic.

The next step is to lay the plastic sheeting in the bottom of the depression where it will completely cover the inside of the hole with about two feet of excess around the perimeter in any direction. Weigh down the ends of the excess plastic with rocks, wood, or other heavy materials to keep it from flapping in the breeze, but don't use any dirt you might have excavated from the depression. Somehow dirt always seems to find its way into the bathwater.

Next, begin the tedious job of filling your bathtub with water. You may need approximately ten gallons. With a quart canteen in one hand and a canteen cup of equal volume in the other, you may need to make about twenty trips before you have enough water in which to bathe.

The only problem at this point is the temperature of the water in the bathtub, which is still uncomfortably cold. There are several ways to bring the water temperature up to a comfortable level, the easiest of these being to simply let the water warm in the sun. On an 80-degree day this will take about three hours. Or you can heat water on the campfire in whatever containers are available—a slow, tedious chore. Large rocks heated near the fire and then submerged in the bathwater are a quicker

The sunken bathtub is for campers and backpackers who need a bath but don't want to freeze their anatomies in frigid, spring-fed streams.

way to get the water temperature up, but they should never be laid directly on the plastic-lined bottom. When using hot rocks to heat bathwater, always set them on top of an item of submerged clothing to keep them from melting through the plastic bathtub liner.

A word of caution here: *never* apply heat to any stones found in the water. A quick submersion is harmless, except that a hot rock might split in two from the shock of suddenly hitting cold water, but stones that have been in the water for a long period of time have absorbed moisture. To heat a *waterlogged* stone can cause tremendous steam pressure to build inside it, which might in turn cause the rock to literally explode with all the force of a hand grenade. Make sure the rocks you use are completely dry.

After you've completed your bath you may want to wash your laundry. It's probably not a good plan to wash cooking utensils in water in which you've just bathed or done your laundry, but a smaller, more easily heated basin makes a great kitchen sink for giving your mess kit a thorough cleaning. Once you've exhausted all the uses you might find for a large (or small) reservoir of warm water, just pull one of the weighted ends of the plastic sheet down into the hole and let the water seep back into the earth.

Finally, it's inevitable that your plastic bathtub liner will develop a hole sooner or later, usually from a sharp object or a hot spark. A leak defeats the purpose of carrying plastic in the first place, yet it seems silly to take elaborate measures to patch it. Fortunately, most leaks can be repaired on the spot with strips of overlapping vinyl electrical tape applied over the hole on both sides of the plastic. The patch need not be strong because in most applications—including the sunken bathtub—there will be little real pressure against the plastic.

The next time you're feeling grimy from carrying a heavy pack all day, treat yourself to a nice warm bath. This sunken tub might not meet the standards of its more civilized counterparts, but after a few days on the trail it will seem as luxurious as any the Hilton has to offer. It sure beats jumping buck naked into an icy stream.

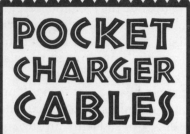

POCKET CHARGER CABLES

MATERIALS NEEDED:

▼

*Heavy 2-conductor
electrical cord, 8' or longer*

▼

40-watt soldering iron

▼

Roll of rosin-core solder

▼

*4 large alligator clips with
rubber boots*

Everyone who drives a motor vehicle will at one time or another experience the problem of having a dead battery. A car that won't start because its headlights, dome light, or ignition was left on is undoubtedly the most common of automotive troubles, and it's a pretty good bet that all of us will need a jump start sooner or later. The problem is that too many folks don't always have a set of jumper or charger cables in their cars or trucks.

The following section describes how to construct a simple pair of light-duty, pocket-sized charger cables that everyone will likely find handy, especially backwoods four-wheelers who frequently drive themselves miles off the nearest beaten track. Simple and inexpensive to make, a pair of these chargers can be stashed in every glove box, toolbox, and junk drawer to make certain that a set will always be on hand. And maybe best of all, they can be made to almost any length desired, so reaching from vehicle to vehicle need not be a problem.

I should point out right away that these chargers *are not intended to cold-jump a dead battery, but are meant to be used for carrying a charge to it from the engine of an idling vehicle.* Assuming that the battery and the vehicle it's in are both in good working order, that will be enough to get the stranded vehicle started under its own power after 15 to 20 minutes of charging. *The chargers should never be used to directly jump start a weak or dead battery* because the current drawn by the starter is more than light-duty wiring can handle and the chargers may become hot enough to melt.

Probably the best wiring to use for making these chargers is two-conductor appliance cord, 18-gauge or larger, preferably with a polarity stripe running alone one conductor (the polarity stripe isn't necessary, but it will help to avoid mix-ups during construction). This wire is heavy enough to carry ample current to the battery under charge, yet small enough to coil a 10-foot length of it into a pocket-sized package. The wire can be purchased in just about any length you desire from most hardware stores.

With the desired length and size of wire in hand, the only components needed to finish the jumpers are four large alligator clips with colored rubber boots. These can be purchased from electronics supply stores for about $1.00 a pair. The insulating rubber boots, two black (-) and two red (+), are needed not to protect you from getting a shock, but to clearly identify the polarity of either conductor at both ends.

To begin, strip about a half inch of insulation from all four ends of the appliance cord and twist the exposed copper strands of each end tightly. For best results, each of the exposed ends should be "tinned" by applying a hot soldering iron to it and melting a small amount of rosin-core solder into the twisted strands. Use only enough solder to turn the wire a silver color and carefully shake off any excess solder while the wire is still hot. In a few seconds the tinned ends will have cooled and become very stiff.

At this point, separate the two conductors of the cord to a depth of about six inches at cither end and slide the colored rubber boots over each wire, making certain that the two red boots are on the same wire. With all four boots installed on the proper conductors, use a pair of needle-nosed pliers to form a small hook in each of the tinned wire ends.

Next, place each of the tinned hooks under the screw terminal on each of the four alligator clips. The screws will tighten in a clockwise direction, so make sure that the end of the tinned hook being attached is on the right-hand side of the screw. This is a standard wiring procedure that ensures the hook will tighten in place as the terminal screw is torqued down. When all four alligator clips have been attached, squeeze the crimp points at the rear of each clip around the insulation of the

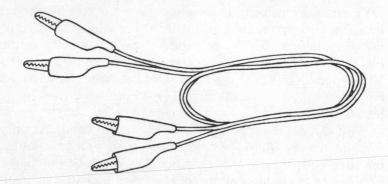

Pocket charger cables, made from large alligator clips soldered onto two-conductor appliance cord, are pocket-sized, inexpensive, and capable of charging any dead battery from a running vehicle.

wire to which the clip is attached and slide the rubber boots over them.

Using the pocket charger cables is very similar to using full-sized jumper cables, except that you can't immediately crank the engine of the vehicle being charged. The alligator clips aren't large enough to attach directly across the battery terminals, but they will clip onto the bolts used to tighten the terminals on the battery posts. Always make doubly sure that the red clips are attached to the positive (+) terminals of each battery and the black clips to the negative (–) terminals. Improperly connecting the two batteries could cause the battery being charged to explode like a small bomb, hurling shrapnel and sulfuric acid in all directions, so be careful.

After allowing the dead battery to charge for about fifteen minutes from the electrical system of an idling vehicle, there should be enough stored energy in it to start the engine. For an added boost, the chargers can be left in place when starting the engine, just so long as the cranking time doesn't exceed more than a few seconds. Remember, the cables might melt if kept in place while cranking for more than a few seconds.

In a few cases, the pocket chargers may be even handier than full-sized jumper cables. Once, after accidentally leaving the lights of my 4×4 on for several hours, I used my 650cc motorcycle to charge its battery until the truck started under its own power. In this instance, full-sized jumpers would have been too large to attach to the 12-volt motorcycle battery without shorting against the bike's frame. But the pocket charger cables worked just fine, and others have reported the same success when using them to start motorcycles, garden tractors, and ORVs (off-road vehicles).

The pocket charger cables are never going to replace my full-sized, extra-long cables, but with so much utility in such compact, inexpensive packages, I now carry a pair of them in the glove box of all my vehicles, the toolkit of my motorcycle, and each of my toolboxes You never know when you're going to have a dead battery, but it always seems to happen right after you've loaned your jumper cables to someone else.

BUMPER JACK WINCH

MATERIALS NEEDED:

▼

Bumper jack (including handle/crank arm)

▼

2 C-type clevis clips

▼

2 50' lengths of 3/8" tow-rated cable with a hook at each end

If you're an avid hunter, angler, or camper, it goes without saying that you'll eventually get your vehicle stuck on the way to some remote location. It doesn't matter how tricked-out your 4×4 is, there will always be a section of two-track road that can immobilize it, and if your boondocking vehicle is a two-wheel drive, having a winch becomes even more of an imperative.

The trouble is that many of the less expensive cable-type "come-along" winches aren't built strongly enough to pull out a really stuck vehicle, and getting one that is will cost you about $300.00. Fortunately, there's an old-timers' solution to this problem that uses an ordinary bumper jack and two lengths of wire cable with hooks at either end to create an extraordinarily powerful winch. The bumper jack winch isn't new, although probably most people have never seen one, but it works very well, is simple to make, and costs under $30.00 in most cases. In fact, if you look around a bit, it might cost nothing.

Functionally speaking, the bumper jack is a pretty remarkable piece of engineering, built to apply a linear force that can be utilized for pulling, lifting, or even pushing, depending upon how it's connected and anchored. When used for winching, the bottom of the jack pillar, which is normally pressed against the ground via the jack base, is left free. Instead, the top of the jack pillar serves as the anchor point, while what would normally be the bumper lift is used to apply a pulling force to the stuck vehicle via a cable or tow rope (see illustration).

Converting a bumper jack to winching duty is as simple as drilling two three-quarter-inch holes through the jack pillar

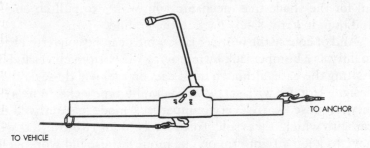

TO ANCHOR

TO VEHICLE

The old-style bumper jacks once sold with every vehicle can easily be converted into powerful winches, capable of pulling a stuck car or truck free with very little effort.

and installing a C-type clevis at both ends. Each clevis should be no less than a half inch in diameter and, in fact, the heavier the better. On the bottom (pulling) end of the jack pillar, the clevis must be installed on the side opposite the jacking handle to serve as a cable guide during winching. The clevis at the top (anchor) end may be installed on either side. As an alternative, the clevis at the anchor end may also be a pin-type, or a clevis-type grab hook can be pinned through the drilled hole. These options serve to make the winch more versatile.

In use, anchor the top of the jack pillar to a tree or another vehicle with a cable or chain to give the winch something to pull against. Then run another cable from the stuck vehicle through the clevis, and hook it to the bumper lift of the ratchet section. When everything is in place, all that remains is to set the direction selector lever to the UP position, insert the jack handle, and ratchet the stuck car or truck free.

If there's a down side to using this winch, it's that the jack will only pull for a distance of less than three feet at one time. In probably most cases, that will be sufficient to get the stuck vehicle onto solid footing where it can move under its own power. But in a situation where more travel is needed, simply winch the vehicle as far as possible, anchor it snugly to keep it from rolling back, and reset the jack for another pull. The bumper jack winch also has an advantage over many come-along winches because it can be operated in reverse, very useful for the shade-tree mechanic who wants to pull an engine and then lower it safely back to the ground.

And of course the bumper jack winch can be converted back to duty as a bumper jack by removing the bottom clevis and installing the base, although most cars on the road these days are designed for use with screw- or hydraulic-type jacks. More's the pity, because nearly every bumper jack made has outlived the car with which it was sold. Fortunately for us two-trackers who have to keep a tight grip on our money, these old workhorses can be saved from the scrap heap by resurrecting them to serve as one of the best overall winches I've ever used.

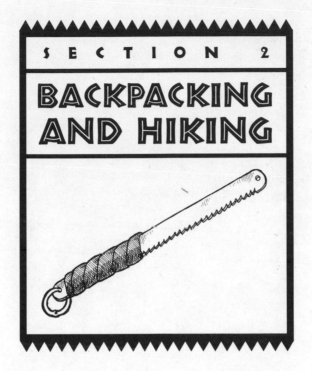

SECTION 2

BACKPACKING AND HIKING

BASIC ORIENTEERING (MAP AND COMPASS)

While I was speaking to the senior class of a local high school recently, a young lady raised her hand and asked if I ever got lost during any of my excursions into the wilderness. When I replied in the negative and added that it was impossible for me to become lost, her reaction was one of utter disbelief. To this young lady and her classmates, it apparently sounded as if I had made the brag of the century and it was tough for me not to laugh at the response my claim elicited from the entire class.

Nevertheless, my assertion was true for two simple reasons: I carry a compass religiously whenever I'm in the woods, complemented by a quality area map, and I understand how to use both of them together. Because of satellites and aerial photography, no place on earth is completely unknown, and topographical maps of state or federal wilderness areas are surprisingly well detailed. Barring injury, a fierce storm, or some other mishap that might make foot travel impossible, no modern woodsman of any discipline will ever become "lost" if he or she possesses a simple compass, a map, and a fundamental knowledge of orienteering.

To the uninitiated, the modern compass can seem a somewhat bewildering piece of equipment, with its numbers, rotating bezel, multiple map scales, and sights. In fact, the only automatic function actually performed by even the most sophisticated compass is that of pointing toward magnetic north. It does this reliably all the time, every day, regardless of which direction the user is facing, but that's all it does. Everything else is up to the user—all the other navigational wonders that can be performed with compass and map are attributable to the user, whose calculations are always based upon knowing in which direction magnetic north lies.

Let's begin by breaking down the compass dial. Most have a single two-color indicator—or arrow—mounted on a pillar in

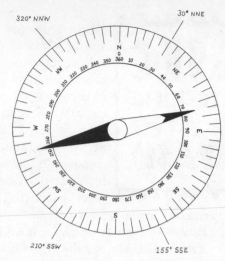

320° NNW

30° NNE

210° SSW

155° SSE

By comparing the compass dial to an analog clock face, outdoorsmen can more easily understand its workings.

the center of the dial (some, like the GI lensatic compass, have a rotating dial). The function of this indicator is to point to magnetic north while its opposite end points to the south. In most cases the indicator half that points north is colored red or orange and the southern half is typically white, but this may not always be true. I've caught more than one beginner in my survival groups plotting a course from the wrong end of his compass, so make certain that you know which half of the indicator points north before you enter the woods.

The outer edge of the compass dial is marked with graduations around its circumference. On smaller "pocket" compasses like the Silva Type 12 or Brunton 9040, these graduations are in five-degree increments, while the more sophisticated map compasses are marked in increments of two degrees or less. But in all cases the number of degrees represented on the dial is 360, which as you might recall from high school geometry classes is the total number of degrees in any circle, regardless of its diameter. It may help to think of the compass dial as a clock face, except instead of having only 60 units representing minutes, the compass has 360 units representing degrees. Just as the number 12 on a clock face is both the end and the beginning of an hour, so is the number 360 (due magnetic north) the beginning and end of the compass dial.

The compass dial further resembles a clock face in that it is divided into four sections, called "quadrants," each of which contains 90 degrees (90 × 4 = 360). The dividing line for each of these quadrants is represented by one of the four compass directions. At 360 degrees (twelve o'clock) is due magnetic north; at 90 degrees (three o'clock) is due east; adding another 90 degrees brings us to due south at 180 degrees (six o'clock); still another 90 degrees brings us to due west at 270 degrees (nine o'clock). And by adding the last 90-degree quadrant we arrive back where we began at 360 degrees. Anyone who can tell time from a standard clock face should have little difficulty making the transition from elapsed time in minutes to direction in degrees.

A somewhat antiquated method of communicating directions via the written word is to further divide each of the four quadrants in half at the 45-degree mark (45 + 45 = 90). A direction is then written using both the number of degrees indicated and an abbreviated reference to its position within a quadrant. For instance, a course direction of 40 degrees might be written as 40 NNE (40 degrees north-by-northeast), meaning that the direction indicated is more north than east. A heading of 200 degrees would be written as 200 SSW. In the days before compasses were mass produced and an outdoorsman was fortunate just to have one that showed the four directions, it was necessary to use ballpark course estimates like west-by-southwest or north-by-northeast. That practice is a bit redundant today, when even a five-dollar compass offers the precision to call out bearings to within five degrees just by reading them directly from the dial, but like the phonograph it continues to be used.

One of the most common mistakes made by even experienced woodsmen is forgetting to take an initial bearing upon entering the woods. The back trail, or return route, will always be in the opposite direction (180 degrees) from the entry trail. A hunter entering the woods at a heading of 35 degrees north-by-northeast will find his back trail by adding 180 degrees to his original heading: 35 + 180 = 215 degrees. If his original heading was a course of 320 degrees, then the back trail will be at 140 degrees SSE (320 − 180 = 140). (When the original heading is equal to or less than 180 degrees, always add 180 degrees to determine the back trail. If the original heading is greater than 180 degrees, subtract 180 from it to find the back-trail heading.) This kind of simple, straight-line navigation will be all most of us will ever require, but remember to take that first, critically important bearing as soon as you enter the tree line.

A step up from the simple pocket compasses are the clear-plastic map compasses like the Brunton 8020, Silva Type 3, or Suunto M3-D. Map compasses range in price from $10.00 to $50.00, depending on the features offered, but all of the quality-made name-brand models have more utility than most of us will ever need.

In practice, the map compass can be used like any compass, by holding it in the hand parallel to the ground and at least a foot away from any ferric metals (if the compass needle is deflected by it, it's ferric metal). To the wilderness explorer equipped with an accurate topographical map who has miles to go, the map compass is far more valuable than a simple pocket compass. Its see-through housing is designed to be laid directly on top of the map so that both compass and map may be oriented together toward north while terrain features can be read through the compass body without removing it from the map. Once a course direction has been determined, the beveled straightedge allows the route to be marked in pencil or crayon and the distance read in either kilometers or miles from one of the built-in map scales along the sides. For navigation through open country, some map compasses also feature rifle-type sights or a flip-up mirror with a single vertical crosshair, or both, for taking accurate bearings from landmarks several miles distant. A few even have integral magnifying lenses to help read the fine, sometimes nearly illegible print on some maps.

A detailed map will complement and enhance the value of any good compass, even if it's just a basic pocket model, by indicating roads, trails, rivers, lakes, and other landmarks, so give some thought to finding the best map available. If nothing else, a state road map from the local Amoco station is better than no map at all, but a detailed topographical map like the ones produced by the US Geological Survey can prevent a lot of heartaches—and maybe heart attacks—by identifying swamps, tall hills, and other types of rugged territory that might best be avoided. State mapbooks published by your state's Department of Natural Resources are a good choice because each map is laid out in a square-mile grid to make coordinate and distance estimation easier and more precise. Trails, roads, fire lanes, lakes, campgrounds, and streams are all clearly identified, as are both national and state forest boundaries. These mapbooks are especially valuable for the serious backpacker, but a few of their maps may be in need of updating and it might be wise to contact the local DNR field office or ranger station before embarking on a hiking trip. I recently attempted to visit remote O'Neal Lake in northern Michigan—practically in my own backyard—only to discover that every vehicle trail leading to it had been posted as private property, even though the map showed them to be public access roads.

Bear in mind, too, that any map carried in the wilderness will eventually be exposed to wet conditions that can reduce it to a clump of useless pulp if it hasn't been protected against the elements. Clear, plastic contact paper, available in most department stores, provides a weatherproof, nearly indestructible lamination for maps and paperback book covers. The Campmor company of Paramus, New Jersey, also lists a product called "Stormproof" in its mail-order catalogue, which will reportedly protect paper maps with an invisible, foldable, waterproof seal that can be written on in pencil or ink. I haven't tried Stormproof, but an eight-ounce bottle of the liquid retails for $6.00 and is said to treat up to 50 square feet of paper. A Ziploc sandwich bag provides additional protection against foul weather and makes a roomy, convenient pouch for carrying maps, a pencil or crayon, and a small spiral-bound notebook for recording coordinates.

You may have noted that previous references to north have been written here as "magnetic north." All compasses point toward the magnetic north pole, which is not in the same place as the "true" north pole, and there are few places in North America where a compass will align with both poles (one of those places is Calumet in upper Michigan's Houghton County). The discrepancy between magnetic north and true north is called "declination" and this discrepancy between the two north poles increases progressively the farther you travel to the east or west of a zero line (where both poles are in agreement) that runs roughly from the southern tip of Florida through the base of Michigan's Keweenaw Peninsula. For example, hikers east of the zero line would have to **add** five degrees to any compass reading if they wanted to obtain a bearing based on true north rather than magnetic north. Hikers near Calumet, Michigan, could read their bearings directly from the compass because their location is right on the zero line where true north and magnetic north are in alignment. In Fairbanks, Alaska (west of the zero line), hikers would have to **subtract** an incredible 35 degrees from their compass readings to find their headings based on true north.

Magnetic Declination Map of the United States

Add the number of degrees indicated on the map to your compass reading if you are east of the zero declination line. Subtract if you are west of the zero declination line.

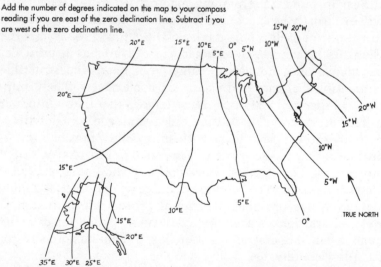

Compasses always point toward magnetic north, which is seldom the same as true north. Cross-country hikers must account for this discrepancy between the two norths if they're to plot an accurate course.

To illustrate how important declination can be, let's put all these numbers into a hypothetical real-life scenario. Let's say a hiker sets out to walk cross-country from point A to point B using a good map compass and a detailed map whose coordinates are referenced to true north, rather than magnetic north. If our hiker fails to compensate for, say, a five-degree declination of his location, he will be more than a half mile east of where he should be after walking just six miles. After 10 miles, he'll be off course by just over 1 mile. If he were trying to locate a cabin in cold weather, failure to account for declination could have serious consequences.

By now this all probably sounds like a lot of trouble. But don't throw your hands in the air and swear off being an outdoorsman, because many of the maps currently printed for use in the out-of-doors are adjusted to compensate for declination. In other words, their coordinates are based on magnetic rather than true north, which allows the wilderness navigator to plot a course directly, without figuring in the declination value. However, not every map is adjusted for declination, especially the older ones, so before using any map for backpacking or hunting make certain that you know which north its coordinates are based on. We've seen how failing to compensate for declination with a map oriented to true north could result in your being miles off course, but accounting for declination with a map based on magnetic north can be at least as bad.

If you don't own a compass and have decided that it might be a good idea to purchase one before your next outing (it is), make your selection as if your life might someday depend upon it (it may). The compasses named here are all of proven reliability and priced within reach of almost everyone. But as with many products, there are a few compasses out there of such poor quality that they don't even merit consideration, so choose carefully. Liquid-filled compasses are the best choice because they don't have the tendency to stick—as do some air-filled compasses—and the liquid provides a good braking action that eliminates needle bounce. Never purchase any liquid-filled compass that has a bubble in the liquid. Bubbles are a sure indication that quality wasn't up to snuff at the factory and a small bubble in a new compass can be counted on to grow into a large bubble that will trap the indicator needle and make taking an accurate reading impossible. The indicator should swing immediately toward magnetic north when the compass is laid on a flat surface, it should settle rapidly, and it should maintain its position without hanging up as the body of the compass is rotated. I also like to see a strongly magnetized indicator needle that will follow a steel paper clip completely around its dial.

On the other hand, there's no need to go overboard when purchasing a compass. The average deer hunter or mushroom seeker can get by very well with a simple pocket compass, while the most dedicated long-distance backpacker will find a good map compass more than adequate. Sophisticated and expensive "pocket transits" like the Brunton 5008, which boasts accuracy to one-sixth of a degree and is designed for use with a tripod, are extreme overkill unless you plan to backpack hundreds of miles through the Amazon rain forest. The folding Brunton 8040 retails for about $50.00 and will meet the navigational requirements of the most demanding recreational outdoorsman anywhere in North America. The rugged, time-proven GI lensatic compass costs about the same, but its "induction-dampened" (air-filled) rotating dial is often maddeningly slow and its aluminum housing doesn't lend itself to use with maps as easily or quickly as do the transparent map compasses.

After you've found the compass that best suits your needs and budget, familiarize yourself with its capabilities and trust it completely. Not believing a compass in the deep woods or swamp is a surprisingly common mistake, particularly when the sun is hidden by cloud cover or foliage. Not long ago a friend who should have known better got himself seriously disoriented in a large cedar swamp when he decided that his compass was lying to him. When he finally emerged onto an old railroad grade, he found that second-guessing his compass had earned him a two-mile walk back to where he should have surfaced in the first place. Unless it has an obvious—and unlikely—malfunction like a large air bubble in the liquid or a stuck indicator, a compass will always point to magnetic north because it simply cannot do otherwise.

At this point, you should have sufficient knowledge of orienteering to help you find your way into and out of almost any forest in the United States. For further information about using the map and compass, I recommend the good old *Boy Scout Handbook* as a great place to start. There are also a number of books and VHS videotapes available for those who develop a yen to learn advanced orienteering techniques, and my own book, *Practical Outdoor Survival*, contains a comprehensive section about using the map and compass to regain civilization under inhospitable conditions. However, most of us will never require more than a solid understanding of the information presented right here to be able to truthfully answer "no" when someone asks, "Do you ever get lost in the woods?"

WEATHERPROOF MAPS

MATERIALS NEEDED:
▼
*1 roll clear contact paper
(usually 18" wide)*

Miserable. That's the only way I can describe the weather. It was my second day in the forest and my second day of being drenched. Since it was early May, the spring rains were cold. They were also very heavy, punctuated by thunder that was sometimes deafening and flashes of lightning so bright that I saw spots before my eyes. My glasses had long since become useless and were riding in my breast pocket. As usual, I was tentless, and my poncho had been committed to keeping my bedroll dry. The previous night had been spent in a shallow cave I'd excavated into the side of a hill. Supper had consisted of cold pork and beans and summer sausage. Breakfast had been ignored.

Yet in spite of being miserable I was thoroughly enjoying the peace and solitude of those water-logged woods. My woolen underwear and socks retained enough body heat to prevent hypothermia, even though they were soaked through. My camera was tucked safely inside a Ziploc bag in my pack. My wool blanket was rolled inside my poncho and dry. All in all, I figured I had everything more or less under control.

By noon I arrived at the river, pretty much on schedule. It was a small river, about thirty feet wide and four feet deep in the middle. The heavy rains had caused it to swell a foot or so and the current was fast, but not dangerously so. Still, I wasn't all that anxious to wade it, which in hindsight was a mistake. After a few minutes of searching I was rewarded with a fallen cedar whose length spanned the river from bank to bank.

But as I began crossing I discovered that the rough bark on the exterior was coming loose from the greasy-slick wood beneath it. Huge raindrops spattered off the brim of my bush hat as I eased across in a sidewise fashion, taking care to keep the rounded surface of the log nestled into the arches of both feet. I'd reached midstream and was feeling pretty good about the whole situation when suddenly my medicine turned bad. The bark under my leading foot slid several inches. I retained my balance on one foot until the bark under that one also slid, sending me backwards into the roaring, foamy waters.

Fear never entered my mind—it was already too filled with rage. Furious, I planted both feet against the bottom and stood up in the cold, neck-high water. Sputtering and cursing, I stomped my way ashore. A quick inventory of my gear showed that I hadn't lost anything, but the streams of water coming from the drain holes in my ALICE pack told me that everything that hadn't been wet certainly was now. Except my camera. That was a relief.

But when I reached for the map I carried folded up in the compass pocket of my harness, I discovered a clump of soggy paper. Try as I might, there was no way to unfold the pulpy, ink-smeared mass. And without the map I hadn't a snowball's chance in Miami of finding the place I was looking for. The trip was at an end.

Depressing, isn't it? Every piece of equipment carried by an experienced woodsman has a purpose. Some are more valuable than others, but any one of these items will be missed if it's lost or destroyed. In this particular instance, my map was very valuable. Without it I couldn't go on.

But I've since discovered a way to protect my valuable maps from the ravages of rain, snow, and high winds. I found the answer in a simple roll of clear contact paper, available for under $3.00 in the home improvement section of most department stores. This stuff was originally intended to serve as a shelf covering in the home, but it also works very well for large lamination jobs—like maps.

For those who haven't used it, clear contact paper comes in a roll 18 inches wide and several yards in length, depending on the size of the roll. The clear polyethylene sheeting has an adhesive on one side and is covered by a removable backing. The backing has a scale printed on it for easy measuring.

To laminate a map, cut two pieces of clear contact paper from the roll about three inches longer than the map. For maps wider than 18 inches, the contact paper may be overlapped without affecting the map's legibility. Next, spread the map on a flat surface (a kitchen table works fine) and peel the backing away from the first four to five inches of plastic. Stick the exposed plastic to both the table and the map. This will hold the end of the contact paper and the map in place while you slowly peel away the rest of the backing. Don't try to stretch the plastic over the map or hold it tight; just let it lay down naturally. This will minimize the number of wrinkles and air bubbles. Rub the heel of your hand over the covered map forcefully to ensure that the adhesive is stuck tight. Now turn the map over and laminate the other side. If you'd like to have a double-sided map, simply lay another map over the first before applying the back sheet of contact paper. Be sure that the plastic lamination extends beyond the edges of the map all the way around. The two pieces of lamination should be stuck to one another at the edges, providing a watertight seal for the map inside.

Finally, trim the outer edges of the plastic to make them look neat and fold the map, creasing it with each fold. You now have a map that's impervious to water and won't rip in a high wind. An added benefit is that the laminated map can be marked on with a crayon or grease pencil. Routes marked with a crayon won't wash off in the rain, yet are easily removed by rubbing a dry cloth over them.

As for me, I haven't gotten any smarter. I still camp in the rain without a tent. And I still fall into rivers on occasion. But with my laminated maps at least I always know where I'm going.

HIKING PACE COUNTER

MATERIALS NEEDED:

▼

1 shoelace, any color

▼

Plastic gas line or similar tubing, 5"

Even with today's precision compasses and detailed topographical maps, any serious attempt at orienteering in a large wilderness requires that a hiker have some method for measuring and keeping track of distances traveled. Locating one tiny objective, like a cabin or hunting camp in a large forest, gives real meaning to that old adage about finding a needle in a haystack. Without the ability to reliably estimate how far you've walked, it becomes difficult to calculate how far you have left to go, or at what point a course change is needed.

Probably the most workable solution to this problem is the abacus-style pace counter used by the US Army. These simple yet very effective pace counters retail for about $5.00 from army-navy stores and mail-order companies, but are so simple to make that buying one seems like a waste of money. I always have several homemade pace counters on hand for camping or hunting companions and it makes sense to me that every piece of gear containing a compass should also carry a pace counter.

For all its value, the pace counter is among the simplest of all projects to complete. Its entire construction consists of nothing more than 13 beads threaded onto a string. The beads are separated into two groups of four and nine beads, separated from each other by a knot. In use, these beads are slid along the length of string holding them, so the string needs to be about three times longer than the total distance covered by the beads in either group. For instance, if the beads used are a quarter inch wide, then the string into which the smaller group of four beads is threaded should be at least three inches in length. By that same standard, the length of string needed for the larger group of nine beads would measure about seven inches.

Any number of methods and materials can be used to make this type of pace counter. My own method uses a shoelace and a five-inch length of plastic tubing (gas line) with an eighth-inch inside diameter. With a pair of sidecutters or a sharp knife, cut the tubing into 13 quarter-inch sections. These are the "beads."

Fold the shoelace in half, bringing the two reinforced ends together, and slide all 13 beads over them and onto the shoelace. When all the beads have been strung, tie a knot in each doubled end of the shoelace to keep them from sliding off. Split the beads into groups of four and nine at either end of the shoelace and separate them with a knot tied at least three inches from the end holding the smaller group.

Other methods of making this device are as varied as your own imagination. I've made pace counters from store-bought beads, buttons on a string, and even split-shot sinkers crimped onto monofilament fishing line. Once I even made a tiny one from doubled carpet thread and beads of insulation stripped from 18-gauge automotive wire. Not surprisingly, I lost that one almost immediately and never did find it again. The only requirements are that the unit be small enough to carry in a pocket and that the beads fit snugly enough on the string to stay where you put them.

Using the pace counter is slightly more complicated than making one, but anyone who can read a map and compass should have no trouble understanding how it works. The pace counter just described is designed to keep track of distance in kilometers rather than miles because the base-10 metric system is simpler. It operates on the principle that an average person's pace will measure 1.5 meters, and 65 paces will equal 100 meters. Beginning with all the beads pushed to the center of the pace counter, a single bead from the larger group is pulled to the end of the cord each time the hiker steps off 65 paces (100 meters).

When all nine beads of the larger group have been pulled to the end, a final 65 paces will bring the total number of paces to 650, which equals one kilometer. At this point, all nine of the beads are returned to their starting position and a single bead is pulled from the smaller group. Another 650 paces, counted off in the same manner as the first, will equal two kilometers traveled,

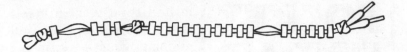

By knowing the length of an average human's pace and keeping track of their own elapsed paces, hikers can calculate distances traveled. The top pace counter has been calibrated for miles and is showing a distance of 1 mile, 600 yards. The bottom pace counter is calibrated for kilometers and shows a distance of 3 kilometers, 500 meters.

and another bead is drawn from the smaller group. When all four beads have been pulled from the smaller group, a final 650 paces will bring the total distance traveled to five kilometers.

Now, if you're one of those folks who just can't get the hang of the metric system, or if your map is scaled in miles, the pace counter can also be made to measure mileage. The only real difference between the two types is that the mileage pace counter has 16 beads in the larger group instead of 9. It works on the idea that 62 paces will equal 104 yards, resulting in one bead being drawn from the large group. When all 16 beads have been pulled to the end, another 62 paces will bring the total distance traveled to one mile, at which point the large group is reset and a bead pulled from the smaller group. Up to five miles can be counted off before the beads of both groups have to be reset.

Whichever you prefer, miles or kilometers, the pace counter is a very handy complement to the map and compass, because probably none of us possesses the single-minded concentration needed to keep count of our paces mentally. But with those three tools—compass, map, and pace counter—and a modest knowledge of orienteering, you'll always know where you're going, where you are, and how far you've traveled. Maybe best of all, you'll be able to find your way back to the same place repeatedly without the aid of a marked trail, which really helps to keep that favorite hunting or fishing spot a secret.

POCKET FIRST-AID KIT

MATERIALS NEEDED:

▼
2-piece plastic soap dish
▼
1 roll white safety tape (½" wide)
▼
1 tube antibiotic ointment
▼
Toenail clippers
▼
Tweezers
▼
Small pair scissors
▼
Small penknife
▼
Alcohol prep pads
▼
Sinus tablets
▼
Ibuprofen tablets or preferred pain reliever
▼
3 or 4 sewing needles
▼
Heavy rubber band, or vacuum cleaner belt

Not long ago a close friend of mine literally set himself ablaze with Coleman fuel during a winter backpacking trip. The injury wasn't nearly as serious as it might have been, but the back of his right hand was covered entirely with horribly blistered third-degree burns that required immediate medical treatment. When a search of his military first-aid kit revealed absolutely nothing useful, I used my home-grown medical kit to treat the wounds with a topical antibiotic cream and analgesic ointment, and then fed him 800 milligrams of ibuprofen for pain. When he did get to a medical facility two days later, the doctor who treated him had only praise for the first-aid care he'd received, particularly since that care had been administered in the unsterile environment of a cedar swamp.

I wasn't surprised; if a truly and entirely functional first-aid kit for woodsmen has ever been manufactured, I haven't seen it. In the wilderness, Band-Aids are useless if they fall off. Gauze, cotton batting, mercurochrome, and probably most of the other equipment you might expect to see in a conventional kit are also of limited value. Worse, most kits generally lack the items a woodsman most needs to stop bleeding, prevent infections, cleanse wounds, and ease pain. I finally concluded that the most *functional* wilderness first-aid kit must be assembled, not bought off a shelf.

The basic first-aid kit I've been carrying in my jacket pockets and survival gear for the past decade begins with a two-piece plastic soap dish. I've found these very useful containers (which I also use for pocket fishing kits and survival kits) priced as low as $.50 apiece ($1.00 is average) at many drug and department stores. They come in a variety of colors and have ample room for the necessities of a working first-aid kit in a compact package that fits easily in a breast pocket. Being so convenient and easy to transport, the kit also eliminates any excuse its owner might have for leaving it behind.

First to go into the first-aid kit is a roll of half-inch-wide white safety tape [a free sample roll is available from General Bandages, Inc., telephone (708) 966-8383]. Safety tape is one of the most versatile products I've found; it sticks tenaciously to itself but nothing else, and it often works better than Band-Aids for bandaging even fairly serious cuts. A full roll of this tape will fit into the soap dish if you first crush its cardboard core and flatten it, but I prefer a more compact form made by rerolling several yards of the tape on a smaller core, such as a short length of Popsicle stick.

Next comes a small tube of antibiotic ointment, such as Neosporin. Doctors generally agree that the most effective way to treat a cut (by far the most common injury in the woods) is to wash it thoroughly, apply antibiotic ointment, and bandage it to protect it from being reopened or exposed to infection-causing foreign material. The old standbys—iodine, betadine, and mercurochrome—are good disinfectants, but they unnecessarily destroy skin cells (that's why using them stings so much) and they don't leave a protective coating over the wound as antibiotic ointment does. With a roll of white safety tape and a tube of Neosporin, you'll have probably 90 percent of the injuries that occur in the wilderness covered.

At this point you'll still have enough space in the soap-dish kit to add toenail clippers, tweezers, a small pair of scissors,

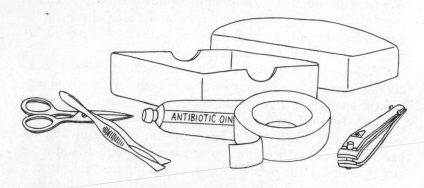

Make an effective pocket-sized first-aid kit by placing small first-aid items into an ordinary plastic soap dish. For more versatility, the entire kit can be inserted into a GI compass pouch and clipped to a belt.

and a small penknife. Even then you should still find room for a couple of alcohol prep pads for cleaning wounds when water isn't available; several blister-packaged sinus tablets; some ibuprofen tablets; and three or four sewing needles sealed between two pieces of cellophane tape. With a bit of adjusting, you'll find a surprising number of small but important emergency medical items can be loaded into this compact container.

To hold the completed kit together through rigorous activities you can use a heavy rubber band, but I've found that a flat vacuum cleaner belt, which resembles a giant rubber band, works better and holds up longer. Or you can forego the rubber bands altogether and carry the kit in a GI compass pouch with attached ALICE clip—my own preference. The packed soap dish slides easily into the compass pouch as though the two were made for one another and the pouch's snap-down flap holds the contents securely. the ALICE clip on the back of the compass pouch rounds out this kit's versatility by allowing it to be fastened to your belt, should that prove more convenient than carrying it in a pocket. GI compass pouches sell for about $3.00 at most army-navy stores, or you can order them from mail-order outlets like U.S. Cavalry, telephone 1-800-777-7732, and Brigade Quartermasters, telephone 1-800-892-2999.

In actual use, the soap-dish first-aid kit has served my companions and myself well more times than I can recall. And in more than a few instances, like the one cited earlier, it has proved more useful than larger commercial first-aid kits costing several times as much. No portable first-aid kit can meet every medical need that might arise, but this one covers most of them efficiently and effectively. In most cases that's enough.

CANTEEN HOT WATER BOTTLE

MATERIALS NEEDED:

▼

Canteen

▼

Hot water (not boiling)

▼

Rag, towel, or shirt

Although the folks who do it regularly will tell you it's always worth the effort, long-distance backpacking sometimes boils down to just plain hard work. Pristine wilderness areas are untracked and untamed because getting to them most often requires considerable effort, and that effort can exact a price. Sore, tired muscles are common the first couple of days out, particularly if your normal workday life is largely sedentary, and nothing can soothe overworked muscles quite like a hot water bottle. The problem is that few experienced backpackers would sacrifice critical space and weight to carry a hot water bottle, regardless of the benefits.

But every backpacker carries a canteen of some type and any of these is capable of performing double duty as a hot water bottle at the end of an exhausting day. Simply fill your canteen with hot (not boiling) water warmed in a mess kit pot and wrap it in a dog rag, towel, or shirt to protect bare skin from being burned and to increase the amount of time that elapses before the water cools. If your canteen is the GI-type with an insulated cover, the entire unit can be used as is, but the newer two-quart GI "water bladder" canteens made from pliable plastic are my first choice. Just apply the insulated canteen directly to sore leg and back muscles for hours of soothing relief.

Winter campers who know that a filled canteen left unattended will turn into a block of ice overnight can also benefit from the canteen hot water bottle, even when sore muscles aren't a problem. A common complaint among winter campers is cold feet during the night, a potentially serious condition be-

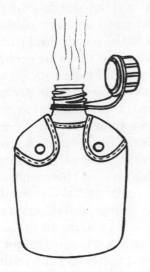

Any type of canteen can serve double duty as a hot water bottle for soothing trail-weary muscles by filling it with hot water and wrapping it in cloth.

cause it robs its victims of restful sleep and wears down the body's resistance to cold and exertion. Placing a wrapped and tightly capped canteen filled with hot water at the foot of your sleeping bag just before turning in will warm up cold, wet feet and may help keep them warm until morning. This technique can be replaced by, or augmented with, a heated rock wrapped in cloth. If you use this method, however, you must exercise an extra bit of caution and common sense. By its nature, rock is a dense material that holds heat for a long time, but it can be made hot enough to ignite clothing and other flammable materials without seeming to be as hot as it really is, so beware. For best results, heat the rock slowly by placing it at the edge of your campfire until the far side of it becomes too warm to hold your bare hand against. And **never** heat a stone taken from a stream or lake bed, because trapped water vapors inside may expand faster than they can escape, causing the rock to explode.

INNER TUBE RANGER BANDS

There are any number of reasons why an outdoorsman might need a heavy rubber band in the woods: backpackers can use them to secure bedrolls and fasten miscellaneous items to their packs; campers can use them for sealing food and other containers against prowling insects and small rodents; bowhunters and photographers frequently find them handy for fastening natural foliage to themselves as camouflage. The uses you might find for a big, sturdy rubber band in the woods, in an infinite combination of circumstances, are limited only by your own ingenuity.

Recently, the United States Army also discovered the usefulness of big rubber bands in the field and gave them the name, Ranger Bands. A package of 10 assorted bands retails for about $3.00 from mail-order retailers like U.S. Cavalry of Radcliff, Kentucky, and Brigade Quartermasters of Kennesaw, Georgia. But before you lay out any hard-earned cash, I recommend first

Although sold commercially, rubber Ranger Bands are made for free easily by cutting sections from various types and sizes of inner tubes. Ironically, the inner tube bands are superior to their manufactured counterparts.

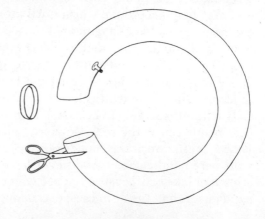

trying the original woodsman's version of the Ranger Band, made from discarded vehicle inner tubes. Bicycle, motorcycle, and automotive tire centers are usually only too happy to let you have their scrap inner tubes, which means everyone can have a variety of heavy-duty rubber bands in the diameters and widths that best suit their needs.

The best tool for converting cross sections of inner tube into nice, straight rubber bands is the big pivoting-blade paper cutter used by schools and offices. But since probably most of us don't own one of these machines, a large pair of sharp scissors or shears will suffice. Fairly straight cuts can also be made with a keen knife by firmly pinning a cross section of the inner tube between two straight boards and using their edges as a cutting guide. Aside from that, I don't recommend using a knife for this project because the rubber is tough and slips are likely.

When cutting out the bands, you'll notice right away that each of them must be cut at an angle to compensate for the greater outer diameter of the tube relative to its inner diameter. Because of that a small portion of the inner tube will be unusable for rubber bands, but that area can be used as patching material.

Once you have a variety of these inner tube Ranger Bands on hand, the uses you'll find for them in the field and at home will be endless. I've used them for boot blousers, wristwatch protectors, field-expedient slingshots, and even to fasten a flashlight to my rifle for hunting at night. And because they cost nothing to make, there's no reason not to have an assortment in the backpack, in the car, and at home.

BACKPACK HACKSAW

MATERIALS NEEDED:

▼
1 hacksaw blade
▼
Safety tape
▼
1 snap-closed (notebook) binder ring

This is a very handy, inexpensive, and easy-to-make tool that's light enough to be included in every backpack and useful enough to warrant carrying. Probably everyone knows that the fine, sharp teeth and hardened steel of a hacksaw blade will cut through even tempered metals around the home and garage, but the blade will also make short work of hard-to-cut wet rope and it easily slices through softer materials like plastic. A survival knife with sawteeth along its spine works well for cutting large notches for snare triggers and shelter frames, yet there are times when a backpacker needs to cut through brittle material or make fine, precise cuts. For those times, nothing serves the purpose quite so well as a hacksaw.

To make the campers' hacksaw more packable, the bulky frame must be left behind. The frame actually contributes little in the field and what it does do isn't worth the weight it adds to a pack. The blade is a bit more wobbly without the frame, but it will still do its job admirably.

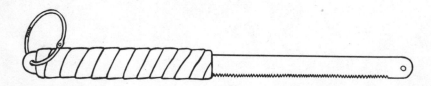

Easy to make and ridiculously simple, a hacksaw blade with half its handle wrapped in tape is one of the most useful tools in a hiker's backpack.

One modification that does need to be made to the hacksaw blade is the addition of a handle to protect the user's hand from being gouged during use. There are a number of ways to accomplish that, but my preferred method is to wrap one half of the blade with several turns of safety tape. The safety tape provides a cushioned, nonslip surface that makes the blade easier to grip. And when the first half of the blade becomes dull, simply unwrap the handle and use the same safety tape to wrap the opposite half, exposing a fresh set of sawteeth in the process.

To conveniently transport the backpack hacksaw, one of my companions came up with the idea of placing a single snap-closed binder ring through the hole at either end of the blade. A binder clip, available from most office supply stores, allows the saw to be clipped through the grommeted holes of a belt, through a belt loop, or through the end of a zipper pull on a backpack, making it more portable and accessible on the trail. Just be careful of the blade, as it may swing or dangle depending on where you hang it.

Although I call this modified saw blade a backpack hacksaw, its uses are by no means limited to backpacking. In fact, this abbreviated hacksaw has so many uses around the home or in your car that you might find yourself using it instead of the full-sized version for most cutting chores requiring a hacksaw. And since the frame is the most expensive part of a hacksaw, you can afford to have several of the backpack variety on hand in each place you might need one.

One day as I was rummaging through my closet in search of the right pair of boots to wear squirrel hunting, I came across my old well-worn GI jungle boots. As I examined these old friends with that special fondness reserved for equipment that has served me well, I noticed they were cracked, badly scuffed, and showed definite signs of abuse. And they had certainly been abused: those boots had probably spent as much time in swamp water as they had on dry land.

In contrast, the boots I selected for wear that day were still soft and supple. Aside from a restitched seam or two, there were few signs that they too had been worn hard, in spite of the fact that they were three years *older* than the jungle boots.

It wasn't quality that made the difference in this instance—not many boots are sturdier than the GI jungle boot—it was the way I'd treated the leather of each pair. The jungle boots had been treated with silicone and other commercial conditioners, like mink oil and "bear grease," while the older, better-preserved boots had been treated with ordinary petroleum jelly. Of the leather conditioning and waterproofing products I've used, none has been as effective or long-lived as petroleum jelly.

If you think about it, petroleum jelly possesses the same qualities as commercial leather conditioners, and so do a good many other greases and oils, including lard. The trick is to get whatever it is you're using down into the pores of the leather where it can do the most good, rather than just smearing it around on the surface where it's sure to be wiped off by mud or snow. The best way I've found of doing that is to heat the leather to open its pores and to liquefy the petroleum jelly so it can be absorbed.

Start by removing the laces from the boots, to allow more access to the nooks and crannies in the tongue area and because heating the laces does nothing to improve their durability. Next, apply a liberal coat of petroleum jelly to the outer surface of each boot, including the tongue area. I think it's especially important to work the grease into stitched seams and along the bottoms where the soles are attached. When both boots have been thoroughly greased, place them on a large cookie sheet.

The next step is to remove the center rack from your range oven and preheat it to 125 degrees. In my experience, this temperature is sufficient to open the pores of the leather without being hot enough to damage vinyl ankle collars or nylon stitching (but keep an eye out anyway, because not all kitchen ovens are calibrated the same). When the oven reaches the desired temperature, place the cookie sheet with the boots on it inside the oven and close the door. After about fifteen minutes, re move the boots and apply another coating of petroleum jelly, especially to the areas that look dry. If the leather is too hot to touch barehanded a rag can be used to work in the second coat of grease. Repeat this process until the leather refuses to absorb any more petroleum jelly, then remove the boots from the oven and work as much grease as possible into the seams while they're still hot.

Leather boots (and gloves) conditioned by this method are soft and accommodating, and new boots will probably require much less breaking in. Saturated with grease, the leather won't dry out or crack even after repeated exposure to water, and stitching will actually last longer because the seams are both lubricated and sealed against the abrasive effects of sand and grit. Nor will that protection wear off easily or quickly; I have one pair of boots that was treated with petroleum jelly more than 12 years ago, and they still repel water like a duck.

Note that I didn't claim this treatment would make your boots waterproof, only that it would waterproof the leather in them. With the limited exceptions of Gore-Tex and similar synthetic materials, any boot material that will keep water out will often hold perspiration in. And no boot is waterproof when you're up to your knees—that's why the GI jungle boot was designed to let water back out, rather than keep it out in the first place. But if you want a pair of swamp-tromping boots that are at least impervious to the damaging effects of water while being as comfortable to wear as they can, baking them with a basting of petroleum jelly is the most effective and least expensive method I've found yet.

SECTION 3

FISHING

MAKESHIFT FISHING LURES

MATERIALS NEEDED:

▼

Fishing hooks

▼

Orange or red yarn, 3"–5"

▼

Parachute cord, ½" lengths

▼

Yellow foam-rubber ear plugs

▼

Colored shoelaces, ½" lengths

▼

Bird feathers

In many wilderness areas of North and South America, fish are a potential source of nutritious and palatable food, which makes a small fishing kit an invaluable piece of life insurance for wilderness travelers. While fashionable survival training techniques include stripping thread from clothing to make fishing line and making hooks from all sorts of things—even a pocketknife—none produces equipment as effective as manufactured hooks, monofilament line, and lead sinkers. A pocket-sized fishing kit (see "Soap-Dish Survival Kit," page 183) is inexpensive and small enough to include on any outing.

But few fish will bite on a bare hook, so bait is a necessity. When worms, grubs, clams, insects, and other natural bait aren't readily available, artificial lures that give the impression of being fish food make the kit ready to use anywhere. My own kits contain scented rubber baits and jigging lures, but knowing how to make fishing lures from other materials can broaden your kit's capabilities and make it more effective.

The simplest type of artificial bait is made from a three-inch length of orange or red yarn tied to a bare hook and floated on the moving surface of a stream or river. It may seem hard to believe that such plain, unadorned bait could work, but colored yarn has become a favorite among sport anglers in pursuit of trout, steelhead, and salmon. Having seen for myself just how effective this most basic of lures can be, I recommend packing several precut lengths of orange or red yarn into any kit that might be used in waters inhabited by these fish.

Any number of effective fishing lures can be made from materials at hand. These six have all caught fish. Top, left to right: surface popper made from a foam ear plug; "parafly" wet fly made from parachute cord; dry fly made from a bird feather and thread. Bottom, left to right: dandelion surface lure; trout and salmon lure made from red or orange yarn; scented shoelace lure.

Another simple, yet effective bait is made from a half-inch length of parachute cord. Every camper and backpacker should carry several yards of this cord in his or her pack. The "parafly" is constructed by first melting the fibers at one end into a rounded mass that simulates an insect's head. The opposite end is then frayed thoroughly to give the fly an animated appearance on the water. Finally, thread the fly over the hook head-first as if it were a worm and toss it into the stream. This bait works well for catching brook trout, bass, and other predatory fish, although you might want to make it a bit longer to attract larger fish.

I've also had some luck using yellow foam-rubber ear plugs to catch bass in the twilight hours before dawn and dusk. I tried this lure a few years ago on a hunch and have included foam ear plugs as part of my fishing kit ever since. Just thread the plug, or a portion of it, into the hook and float it on the water over a likely bass habitat. Largemouth bass seem especially taken with this bait, presumably because it resembles a bumblebee.

Several years ago I met an old-timer who was particularly good at persuading catfish and bullheads to bite. As it turned out, the bait that brought him so much success was nothing more than a two-inch length of colored shoelace saturated with bacon grease. Essentially scavengers, catfish (as well as crayfish and carp) are attracted to the scent, while the color and motion of the shoelace provide visual stimuli. By substituting commercial scent lures for bacon grease, this lure will also work on bass, bluegills, and perch. An added benefit is that the shoelace is practically impossible for smaller fish to disengage from the hook, making it an excellent choice for inland lakes inhabited by "bait stealers."

Nor should you overlook natural materials when conjuring up lure ideas. Discarded bird feathers left behind during preening can be cut into sections and threaded over a hook to make an effective dry fly for trout or bass. Brightly colored flowers will also work in a pinch, and I've caught several bass on simple dandelions.

Whatever type of lures you choose to include in your own fishing kit, I recommend packing along a bottle of liquid fish food scent to make them more attractive. Even though the more predatory fish like perch, pike, and trout hunt largely by visual stimuli, most also possess a keen sense of smell for locating food at night. A few drops of attractant on any of the artificial baits mentioned here can only improve their effectiveness, and when you're fishing for your supper, every little bit helps.

Each of the makeshift fishing lures described here has proved its worth over the years. But as any sport-fishing addict can tell you, no lure will catch fish all the time, so it pays to think innovatively. I once wrapped an old-style beer-can pull tab dropped in the woods by a careless outdoorsman around the shank of my fishhook after running out of worms, a tactic that earned me three more fish. And I've often wondered if fluorescent vinyl flagging tape, which I carry for marking trails, wouldn't work as a fish lure, but I haven't had occasion to try it yet. As with anything, you're limited only by your imagination.

PILL-BOTTLE FISHING FLOATS

MATERIALS NEEDED:

▼

*Empty pill bottle,
or similar canister*

▼

*Heavy rubber band,
or vinyl tape*

▼

Colored tape

Here's another of those projects that works so well it makes me wonder why anyone would spend good money to buy its mass-produced counterpart. As the name implies, pill-bottle fishing floats are made from pill bottles, easily obtained commodities in this age of in-house pharmacies and over-the-counter miracles. Most any type of pill bottle will work to make a bobber so long as it has a watertight seal when the cap is snapped on or screwed down. The narrow-necked type, which has a mouth smaller than its body diameter, is my personal preference for reasons that will soon be apparent, but 35mm film canisters, vitamin bottles, and prescription medicine bottles will all work to catch fish.

The key to making plastic bottles function as fishing floats is to secure the fishing line to the bottle in such a way that it will neither fly off during casting nor slide along slippery monofilament line. I've used vinyl tape and other methods to accomplish that in the past, but the most effective way I've found to secure the line at the desired depth is with a heavy rubber band. Any rubber band will work in a pinch, but my favorites for this application—and many others as well—are made from cross sections of bicycle inner tube cut in half-inch widths (see "Inner Tube Ranger Bands," page 76).

To use the pill-bottle fishing float, first pass the doubled fishing line through the rubber band at the desired fishing depth. The line will emerge on the opposite side of the rubber band as a loop. Wrap this loop around the outside of the rubber band one time and then back through its center, where it will again emerge as a loop. Place that loop over the narrowest part of the bottle (here's where narrow-necked bottles work best). Finally,

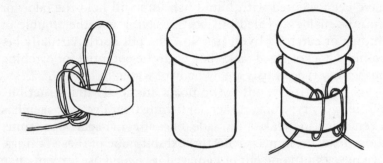

Almost any airtight plastic film or pill bottle can be converted to a "pill-bobber" by looping fishing line through and around a rubber band, and then sliding both line and rubber band over the body of the bottle. As a bonus, tackle can be carried safely inside the bottle, making this a complete pocket tacklebox.

lock the line in place by stretching the rubber band over the bottle body and sliding it up to the cap. A forceful pull on either end of the fishing line finishes the job by tightening the line around both bottle and rubber band. In practice, this entire operation can be performed in just a few seconds. Should you decide to fish at a different depth, it's a simple matter to reverse the procedure and make any necessary adjustments in almost as little time as a conventional bobber would take.

To make a film bottle float more visibly against the water it sits on, I like to wrap a single strip of brightly colored vinyl tape around the bottom of the bottle. When a fish nibbles the bait it will pull the top of the bottle down, causing the bottom to rise out of the water. Any color tape will serve this purpose so long as it contrasts with the color of the bottle being used; but white, yellow, or orange is much easier to see under twilight conditions than a darker color. Vinyl tape can be found in a variety of colors at most hardware and department stores.

Nor does the utility of the "pillbobber" end there. Survivalists and other outdoorsmen who like to hedge their bets against the unexpected can fill the bottle with a coil of monofilament fishing line, an assortment of hooks, some split-shot sinkers, and a variety of small baits and jigging lures. Rubber baits that have been scented with liquid fish lure will hold the odor for months inside a sealed pill bottle, saving you the trouble of finding or catching live bait. Now the pill bottle virtually becomes a pocket-sized tacklebox with the potential for catching nearly any type of fish in any body of water.

As a final irony, pill-bottle floats are nearly indestructible. While every type of commercial fishing float I've ever seen has a tendency to break, sink, fade, or just come apart over time, those made from plastic bottles exhibit none of these failings. I've never worn one out or damaged it beyond use (except once when I lost the cap), even though many have been subjected to considerable abuse on backpacking trips. Inexpensive as they are, it seems like a waste of money to buy manufactured bobbers when I can have a much better-made fishing float at no cost whatsoever.

BOAT ANCHOR BAG

MATERIALS NEEDED:

▼

1 denim pants leg

▼

Darning needle and carpet thread

▼

3' light rope

Probably the most popular reason to buy a boat or canoe made of aluminum is weight— or rather, lack of it. A lightweight aluminum boat doesn't need a cumbersome trailer and it can be launched from almost any shoreline, making all but the most remote fishing holes easily accessible. And if necessary, a single person can carry the craft over considerable distances to get to those fishing holes.

The only real drawback to the lightweight boat is its anchor, which is by definition heavy and ungainly. Carrying a clumsy 10- or 20-pound anchor almost defeats the purpose of a lightweight boat, especially when portaging the craft overland. Yet an anchor is a necessary evil in places where currents or wind can make staying over that favorite fishing hole nearly impossible without one.

The most workable solution I've found to this problem is a simple device I call the anchor bag. Essentially nothing more than a large bag constructed of heavy cloth, the anchor bag is very light and folds compactly enough to be stuffed into your hip pocket. It doesn't become an anchor until you reach the shoreline, where you fill it with rocks, gravel, or even sand to give it the weight needed to hold a boat stationary on the water.

Anchor bags can be sewn completely from scratch, but anyone who makes cut-off shorts will probably find the additional work unnecessary. A heavyweight denim pants leg is nearly ideal for this project because it's already in tube form and all that remains to do is sew the bottom closed. To do this, turn the pants leg inside out and roll the cut end over on itself twice to form a strong hem that closes the bottom securely. A double

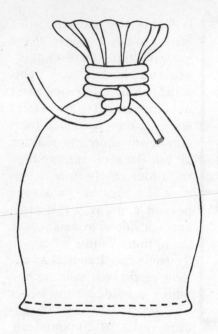

Made from a cut-off pants leg, the anchor bag can be rolled into a small package and carried to the shore. Fill it with rocks or sand to create a heavy anchor.

row of stitches sewn into the hem will hold it together against the bumps and scrapes of being dragged along a river or lake bottom.

With the hem sewn completely shut, turn the bag right side out and sew the rope to its outside, about two inches below the opening. With the rope securely attached, the anchor bag is ready for use. Just fill it with rocks or gravel and wrap the ends of the rope tightly around the bunched mouth of the bag in opposite directions with at least two turns. Tie the ends off with a snug square knot, attach the weighted bag to the anchor line, and toss it overboard.

The filled weight of the anchor bag will of course depend on how large it is and the volume of the material used to fill it. The same bag filled with sand will weigh more than it would if gravel or rocks were used. But in most cases a single anchor bag will weigh in excess of 15 pounds, sufficient to hold a lightweight boat on relatively calm waters. For heavy currents or strong winds, two anchor bags, one at the bow and one at the stern, may be needed. Fortunately, the very light weight of an empty anchor bag makes it easy to carry several, and you just might find (as I have) that the anchor bag makes that heavy manufactured anchor nothing more than dead weight.

JUGGING FOR FISH

Probably the oldest and most prevalent image of a "hillbilly" is that of a shiftless person who works as little as possible, doing no more than what is absolutely necessary to survive. From the works of Mark Twain to Mountain Dew sodapop, a classic portrait of the backwoods ne'er-do-well has often been one of a poor but content, barefooted fisherman lying on a shore with his fishing line and float tied to one toe.

In recent times, hillbillies have been forced to secure proper employment to obtain necessities like automobiles and microwave ovens—items which further promote laziness. The energy-saving fishing methods of yesteryear have also undergone a few changes. Nowadays backwoods fishermen, having benefitted from advances in technology, use a method known as "jugging" to put fresh fish on the dinner table in a manner as efficient as possible. Toes are no longer needed for anchoring the fishline, leaving the rest of the body free to go punch a time-clock somewhere.

Jugging gets its name from the fact that it employs empty plastic jugs, most notably white gallon-size bleach jugs, as fishing floats to keep supper securely hooked until it can be retrieved. Jugging is legal, although some local restrictions (like marking your name and address on the jug) may govern its practice, so be sure to check these first. It's especially effective for species like bullheads, catfish, and suckers, but I've also caught bass, perch, and bluegill with jugs—all while I was off doing something else.

To begin, you'll need a tightly capped, empty plastic bottle, large enough to prevent a large fish from pulling it underwater. Most juggers prefer bleach bottles because their white color is easy to see even at night, and these typically have handles molded into them. I prefer half-gallon bleach jugs to gallon-size because they have enough buoyancy to hold the largest fish and you can carry twice as many in the same amount of space.

Rinse out several empty jugs and tie them together through their handles with a rope (to make transporting them more convenient). All that's needed to complete the jugging outfit are an equal number of hooks and large split-shot sinkers, bait, and a spool of monofilament fishline. Like conventional pole fishing, the size and type of tackle used should conform to the size and type of fish you seek. I think hook size is strictly a matter of preference, but I prefer ten-pound test line, or even heavier, just in case a really big one comes along.

Bait selection also depends on where you are and the kind of fish found there. For bass, perch, and even pike, some juggers prefer to use live minnows. Catfish hunters will generally opt for sourdough (store-bought bread dough mixed with cornmeal seems to work equally well), and others, like myself, have found that plain old nightcrawlers work on just about everything.

Once you arrive at the shoreline of your favorite lake or pond, attach a length of fishline with hook, sinker, and bait to the handles of your jugs. Again, the amount of line used will depend on how deep the water is and the depth at which your prey is most likely to feed. Four feet is usually a good rule of thumb. The line should be securely tied to the jug handle using a standard fisherman's knot (see illustration).

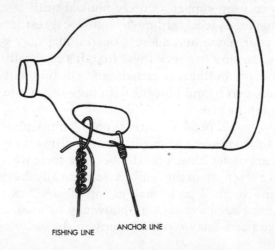

FISHING LINE   ANCHOR LINE

Next, tie a second line around the jug handle to serve as the anchor line, the line that will keep a hooked fish from making off with your outfit. Anchor lines should be at least thirty feet long to allow the fish some room to run, thus helping to ensure that the hook will be firmly embedded. They can be made from fishline, or if you prefer, any stout string or cord can be used. Tie the free end of the anchor line off to a convenient sapling or a stake driven solidly into the ground as near the water as possible.

The final step is to cast the jug out onto the water. Some juggers will do this from a rowboat; however, the simplest method is to coil the baited line into your palm, hook a finger around the jug handle, and toss both as far from shore as you can get them. With that accomplished, there's nothing more to do except wait. Set the remainder of the jugs in the same way, making certain to keep sufficient space between each set to prevent a struggling fish from tangling them together.

The beauty of jugging is that you don't need to hang around until a fish bites; in fact, this technique works best if the angler leaves a biting fish alone for several hours. A hooked fish will be unable to pull the jug underwater, but it will try running, with the jug bobbing along behind like a ball-and-chain. The anchor line will restrict how far it can travel, and provides a means of hauling hooked fish to shore when the angler comes back.

HOW TO FILLET FISH

When I was growing up in northern Michigan, B.C. (before condominiums), there were enough really good fishing holes to allow every angler an opportunity to claim one as his own "secret" spot. There were fewer people, more wilderness, and the big fish hadn't yet been given nervous disorders by dragster-class fishing boats, sonar devices, or seek-and-destroy guided lures. All an angler needed to fill a stringer were a can of worms, a pocketful of hooks and sinkers, and a more or less functional rod and reel outfit—the latter being optional.

For kids, learning to clean and butcher game or fish was a part of growing up that began the day a youngster brought that first catch home for the family dinner table. There were a lot of different aspects to that rite of passage, but a kid who could take a razor-edge knife and present mother with two boneless top fillets from each fish had truly mastered the ancient art of cleaning fish. Mastery was its own reward, because every minute spent cleaning one's catch was time that might be better spent fishing, so it wasn't unusual to see ten-year olds who wielded their folding fish knives with the expertise of a sushi chef.

Filleting fish is a simple task that anyone can do well on the first attempt, given a good set of instructions. Most meat on a fish's body is concentrated in large back muscles (the equivalent of "tenderloins" in other animals), that extend from the head to the tail. These muscles reach roughly from the dorsal fin down about halfway to the belly on either side of the spine and together make up what are known as fillets. With the skin removed, the demarcation between boneless fillets and bone-filled meat is visible as a longitudinal line running the full length of a fish's body on either side. On many fish, like salmon or trout, this line is visible on the skin itself.

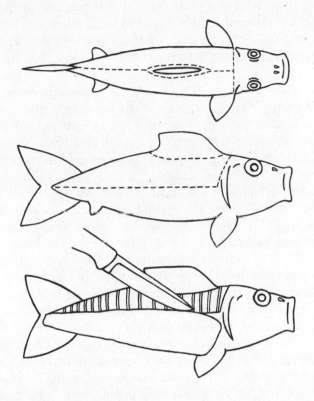

To begin, you'll need a sharp, thin-bladed knife. Fillet knives are of course ideally suited to the task, but pocket, boning, and even paring knives are all capable of doing a fine job. The first step is to remove the scales if that is necessary (i.e., bass, perch, and bluegills), or to remove the skin (catfish, bullheads, and salmon). There's no need to gut the fish or remove its head during the filleting process.

Next, make an incision along the top of the spine, cutting around the dorsal fin(s) on either side. Separate the flesh on one side with a thumb and begin slicing the thick meat away from the ribs using the tip of your knife. Begin at the head and work the fillet loose along the length of the fish's body, until you can feel small bones protruding from the flesh. Slice the fillet off just above the point at which the bones protrude, removing a slab of firm, boneless meat. Repeat this process on the other side of the dorsal fin. When you're finished, you'll have two strips of firm, boneless meat that are ideal for just about any fish recipe, from simply frying them in a pan to baking to fish stew.

There are a few species of fish, most notably those in the sucker family, that have bones in the top fillet portions of their bodies. Sucker meat is, in my opinion, at least as tasty and nutritious as trout, but the proliferation of tiny bones throughout makes it impossible to produce boneless fillets with the process just described. Canning with a pressure cooker will soften those bones to the point of edibility, and smoking will allow the tiny Y-shaped bones to be plucked out easily, but using the meat for other recipes will require a bit of extra work.

The best procedure I've found for getting the bones out of sucker fillets is to first remove the top fillets as described, then slice each fillet lengthwise. From there, the de-boning operation becomes a simple, if tedious, chore of feeling for each small bone with the fingertips, and then plucking it out of the meat. Be warned, however, that this method is not foolproof, and it's likely a few small bones will be missed. Choking probably isn't a concern because the bones are so tiny, but I can tell you from personal experience that being painfully stabbed in the gums, tongue, or throat will demonstrate why many anglers regard the otherwise tasty sucker as inedible.

SECTION 4

HUNTING

THE WELL-DRESSED HUNTER

Hunting the always-challenging white-tailed deer in the north woods frequently means spending many hours outside in temperatures that may range from mildly cool to below zero—sometimes well below zero, if you factor in the wind chill. Yet the deer are still there, going about their normal routine of feeding, breeding, and bedding down, in all but the fiercest storms because they have no other place to go. They might seem as mythical as unicorns when you're facing into blowing snow from a 20 MPH wind on a 20-degree Fahrenheit day (a wind-chill factor of –10 degrees Fahrenheit), but patience and perseverance are key ingredients in any formula for success. And the extent to which a hunter possesses those qualities will often be determined by how well his or her clothing suits the environment.

Most hunters who dress inadequately for weather conditions get off lightly with no more than a mild chill and maybe frostnip. But too many winter outdoorsmen have suffered severe, even fatal hypothermia after being forced to spend a night in temperatures that can plummet more than 40 degrees, discounting wind-chill effects, from their daytime highs. The always real possibility that a hunter might be injured or trapped by a sudden storm is probably the most important reason to dress warmly, but it follows that one who dresses for an indefinite stay in the woods will be warmer and more comfortable even if never faced with such a dilemma. It's a big plus if you're not shivering behind the trigger when the venison finally shows up.

The first step in putting together an effective cold-weather outfit is to realize the popular myth that one has to be completely dry to stay warm is not true. Each of us has been conditioned practically from birth to associate being wet with being cold and sick. Certainly none of us reached adulthood without being told we'd "catch our death of pneumonia" if we didn't "have enough sense to come in from the rain." No one should ever willingly allow him- or herself to become wet, because moist clothing definitely has a cooling effect on the body, but staying both completely dry and warm in subfreezing weather is an ideal situation that often doesn't happen in real life.

Perspiration is the most common offender because parts of the body sweat to some extent constantly, which explains why the liners of the finest sno-pac boot will be damp after a relatively inactive day of ice fishing or snowmobiling. From this standpoint, there's no such thing as waterproof clothing or footwear because (with the limited exceptions of Gore-Tex and other breathable, waterproof synthetics) almost any material that will keep moisture out will also keep it in.

The answer to this dilemma is a material that "breathes" well enough to dissipate perspiration moisture, yet insulates well enough to keep precious body heat from going with it. The answer is wool. Despite innovations like Thinsulate and Hollofil, the all-around favorite cold-weather garment material among many experienced outdoorsmen continues to be old-fashioned natural wool, sometimes mixed with cotton, or synthetic fibers like polypropylene. With its limited ability to repel water, wool clothing dries quickly, breathes very well, and provides superior insulation under even wet, miserable conditions. One of the best endorsements for wool that I've heard is the story of a lucky fisherman who fell through thin ice on Grand Traverse Bay in northern Michigan a few winters ago. The victim, dressed almost entirely in wool, was rolled through the snow immediately after being pulled from the water to squeeze the moisture from his clothing and was able to continue fishing, embarrassed but none the worse off for what might well have been a tragic experience.

Thinsulate is the most recent and probably the most successful synthetic material to challenge wool on the cold-weather clothing front. Like practically every other material with good insulating properties, including foam rubber, fiberglass home insulation, and wool, Thinsulate retains heat by trapping motionless "dead" air within its fibers. Still air is a poor conductor of heat, so warmth generated by the body tends to stay put rather than radiate outward. Thinsulate does breathe well, but practical applications are currently limited to lining garments made from other, more durable materials.

Gore-Tex's ability to breathe, to dissipate perspiration moisture from within while being windproof and water-repellent from without, has made Gore-Tex outerwear popular among recreational outdoorsmen in any season. The unique one-way wicking action of Gore-Tex provides maximum transfer of perspiration or other moisture from inside, which means that clothing worn under it stays drier and wet clothing underneath it dries quickly. But an increase in dissipated moisture carries with it an increased loss of body heat, so heavy perspiration is still a hazard that should be avoided. Marks against Gore-Tex outerwear are its high price and the loss of its special properties with time, use, and regular laundering.

The legs are an often overlooked body area with a high volume of blood flow and a potential for serious loss of body heat. Again, the key to preventing body heat from being lost lies in maintaining a dead air space between the skin and an outer shell of windproof clothing. A dead air space between layers of clothing serves the same purpose as the dead air space in an attic, retaining heat by impeding its escape. Snug-fitting jeans, even when worn over insulated drawers, will allow direct loss of body heat into the cold air, but a pair of baggy, dense-weave trousers (like the US military BDU trousers) worn over woolen underdrawers will resist the cooling effects of a 30 MPH wind while trapping a layer of warmed, relatively motionless air between themselves and the wearer's legs.

For the hunter (or ice fisherman) who plans to be in the field all day in frigid, windy weather, I very much recommend the German military-issue wool six-pocket trousers. These loose-fitting, wonderfully warm field trousers are made from two layers of dense wool with a waterproof liner sandwiched between at the knees and seat, making it possible to kneel or sit on top of the snow without getting soaked through. The intentionally baggy fit provides a generous layer of warmed dead air while the heavy wool construction defeats wind chill and wicks away perspiration moisture. To ensure a comfortable, draft-free fit, the waistband is adjustable both inside and out, the cuffs close snugly around the ankles with either snaps or a drawstring, and the button fly is double-walled. Many army-navy stores have the German wool trousers in stock, or they can be mail-ordered from U.S. Cavalry of Radcliff, Kentucky, for $25.00 per pair.

At least as critical as any other cold-weather garment is a warm, comfortable pair of boots. The feet are always prone to suffer most severely from the cold because of their constant physical contact with the earth; and because they're extremities, farthest from the heart, it pays to treat them kindly. Frostbitten toes are excruciatingly painful, and frozen toes will effectively cripple their owner, sometimes for life. In subfreezing weather, the traditional insulated leather "hunting boot" just isn't enough to keep the toes of a motionless hunter warm. Even if there's no snow on the ground, I recommend wearing a quality sno-pac boot when hunting in temperatures below 32 degrees, particularly if you'll be spending hours sitting motionless in a blind.

When selecting a sno-pac boot, the price tag should have as little importance as your budget will allow. There are an awful lot of makes and models of pac boot on the market, so choose carefully because you'll have to live with your choice in the field. An extra $20.00 or $30.00 can seem a pretty paltry sum when your toes are numb with cold, your feet are cramped from walking with no arch support, or your heels are blistered, so try to find the boot that best suits both your needs and your means. Canvas military "mukluks" retail for about $60.00, are very warm, and provide tennis shoe–like comfort, but don't stand up well to kicking around in the backcountry. The Sorel Dominator boot, described in one field test as "preposterously warm," retails for $130.00, and has an aggressive lug sole and the toughness you'd expect in a Sorel. The LaCrosse Iceman retails for about $120.00 a pair and while not well suited for hiking, the Iceman earns its name in the bitter cold. Military-issue "Mickey Mouse" boots are very warm and rugged, have adequate traction in snow, and offer the unique advantage of built-in wetproof liners sandwiched between walls of tough rubberized fabric. They retail at around $100.00. These prices are averages and a smart shopper will probably be able to beat them all.

The efficiency of just about any pac boot can be further improved at home. Installing hand-cut insoles made from shag carpeting or dense-cell foam rubber in the bottom of each boot over a layer of pressed aluminum foil will noticeably reduce the amount of heat lost through the soles. "Toecaps" made from aluminum foil pressed around the toe of each liner and duct-taped in place will likewise reflect much of the heat that would otherwise be lost from that especially critical area. Don't wear plastic bags over your feet; they provide no insulation and will in fact make the feet wet by trapping perspiration. Nor should you wear more than two pairs of heavy socks at once. Wearing extra socks does little to enhance the warmth of your boots and each additional pair squeezes the feet ever more tightly, causing them to become cold from poor circulation. The large dead air space in a pac boot's toe box is an efficient insulator, but if you want maximum warmth during the time spent on station, open the front of each boot and slide a small, activated chemical handwarmer packet into the toe area between the liner and boot.

Socks, too, have undergone considerable improvement over the years and today's cold-weather socks scarcely resemble the scratchy, knit woolies worn by our fathers or grandfathers. One of the warmest socks I've tried in recent years, and also one of the least expensive, is the wool hybrid sold in major department stores under the Winchester label. I liked them so much I bought six pairs. For those who like the convenience of shopping by catalogue, Cameron Woolens of Sheboygan, Wisconsin, offers a quality line of "specialty" socks for hunting, hiking, and other outdoor activities. It has wool socks, wool-blend socks, polypropylene liners for wicking perspiration away from the skin, and even hybrid socks made from wool and Hollofil, with prices ranging from about $6.00 to $12.00 per pair.

Next on the list of body parts most likely to be affected by cold are the fingers, primarily because these extremities are necessarily exposed to the open air more often than any other part of the body. An ambient temperature of 10 degrees and a wind speed of 10 MPH affect exposed skin the same as would a –9 degree temperature on a windless day. Even this relatively mild scenario is sufficient to reduce unprotected hands to numb, frostbitten claws in only minutes.

Mittens are warmer than gloves because they allow the meager amounts of heat generated by the fingers to combine, rather than isolate each digit the way gloves do. Yet most hunters prefer gloves because having the fingers free will allow them to perform many tasks that the cumbersome mittens won't. Modern hunting gloves with a Gore-Tex shell over Thinsulate provide superior warmth, but are bulky enough to require removal when digging in a pocket or working a firearm. Military-type gloves with leather shells and removable wool liners (my own preference) are windproof and light enough to allow an accurate trigger pull, but in negative temperatures I often find it necessary to sit on my hands to keep them warm. Lightweight wool glove liners worn under warm mittens are a happy medium because the mittens can be removed quickly while the liners provide an acceptable degree of both dexterity and protection.

Any cold-weather ensemble should begin with a good, warm hat. An estimated 15 percent of total body heat is lost from an unprotected head, so keeping your head and face warm will actually help to keep your entire body warm. Some medical research has determined that allowing the nose to become cold causes the germ-trapping cilia in the nostrils to go dormant and greatly increases the probability of contracting a cold. The nose and cheeks are also usually the first areas of the head to suffer from frostbite. A warm hat over the head and ears can be worn with a scarf wrapped around the nose and mouth to provide maximum protection against the cold, but a knit ski mask or balaclava will be adequate in most any weather and can be worn like a watch cap in warmer temperatures.

One nonclothing item that I carry religiously when I'm hunting is a small daypack loaded with cold-weather accessories like spare socks, an extra sweater, a fire-starting kit, chemical handwarmers, a space blanket, an extra compass, a map, and a flashlight. In deference to my affinity for eating, I make certain to stock the little pack with plenty of cheese, peanut butter, and other snacks rich in proteins and complex carbohydrates to keep the metabolic furnace stoked. The day-pack also provides a convenient place to carry garments too warm to wear while walking, and it even makes a pretty good seat during a long wait.

With good luck, good weather reports, and good sense (I wouldn't bet on the first two), none of us will ever need to survive for more than a day in the winter woods. But the ability to survive a cold-weather emergency is just one of the dividends gained from dressing as if for an indefinite stay. For us hunters, the advantage of wearing an effective cold-weather outfit is that it extends the time we can stay in the woods, and that alone can be enough to swing the odds in our favor. Well-dressed hunters will still be on station, warm and snug long after their lesser-dressed compadres have been forced out by the cold. And when that sly old buck finally makes an appearance, they won't miss because they're shivering or their trigger fingers are numb.

HAMMOCK GHILLIE SUIT

MATERIALS NEEDED:

▼

Nylon-netting hammock

▼

Natural vegetation (or cloth strips)

Among wildlife photographers, military snipers, biologists, and other professional outdoorsmen who make their living by blending into the countryside, the "ghillie suit" is the number-one choice in camouflage. Named for the Scottish servants ("ghillie" is Gaelic for "servant") who once wore them to catch poachers on their masters' lands, ghillie suits have proved to be the ultimate camouflage for every type of terrain except possibly urban and snow-covered. Nor have the advantages of ghillie-type camouflage gone unnoticed by sport hunters, especially bowhunters, for whom success often hinges on being as near to invisible as possible.

But manufactured ghillie suits are expensive—about $120.00 for the set, which seems a bit unreasonable for ragged-looking clothing made from nylon netting and strips of cloth. Moreover, these suits are a pain to wear in brush because they snag on everything, making it necessary to carry them in a bundle to your destination, and in warm weather they're oppressively hot. Fortunately, there is an inexpensive and equally functional alternative that makes use of something many of us already carry in our backpacks: a compact hammock made from nylon netting.

Converting the mesh hammock to a ghillie suit—actually more like a ghillie poncho in this instance—is very simple and arguably produces a garment even more effective than those made from camo netting because it uses natural vegetation from the surrounding countryside. Grasses, ferns, and even corn leaves can be woven into the mesh to create a literal blanket of undergrowth with an irregular outline and colors that exactly match the terrain you'll be hunting. With a little effort,

By weaving vegetation into the mesh of a lightweight hammock, hunters and photographers can create a blanket of camouflage that makes them invisible from as little as 25 feet.

just a few minutes, and no practice at all, a varmint hunter can become virtually undetectable from as little as 25 feet in an open field. Being under cover, so to speak, allows him to occupy high ground where tall grasses won't interfere with his ability to shoot from the prone position. I like this method because a rolled baseball-sized hammock is much lighter to pack than prefabricated ghillie material of the same dimensions; because camouflage is usually readily available (and always of the right colors); and because sometimes I like to sling my hammock between two trees at camp and just swing in the breeze.

Net hammocks can also be converted into a more permanent ghillie-type camouflage that will be effective in most types of terrain by tying on strips of neutral-colored cloth and weaving them through the netting. Strips of tan and olive drab burlap, available in roll form at army-navy stores, are excellent for this application, but almost any drab green, gray, brown, tan, or black strips of cloth will do the job. Mosquito netting also works great for this purpose. Just make sure to use rags that are scent-free and laundered with a detergent that doesn't have ultraviolet brighteners. And be sure to leave two to four inches of each strip's free end loose on what will be the outside because ragged, indefinable contours are what makes ghillie camo so effective. You can still use your hammock as a hammock after this operation, but it will weigh about four times as much and will be a little less convenient. This method works especially well for hunters who shoot from a treestand.

The color of the hammock used in this project has little bearing on its effectiveness because by the time you've added enough camouflage materials to cover its surface, even white mesh is all but invisible. Having said that, I still prefer olive drab netting, or at least white mesh that's been turned gray by rubbing it in the dirt. It's probably not a good idea to use spray paint, however, because this imparts a lasting odor to the hammock that could scare off game animals.

The ways you can employ the ghillie hammock are limited only by terrain and your own imagination. One photographer I know likes to climb a tree and sling his hammock between its branches, but this doesn't provide a stable enough platform for hunting and should be discouraged as being too dangerous in any case. Hunters who like to stalk open woods can wear their camouflaged hammock as a poncho by draping its center edge over the head, hood-fashion, and tying it together under the chin. Or you can simply drape it over yourself cape-fashion to form a camouflage blind in most any location you choose to hunt.

Effectiveness aside, one of the biggest attractions of the hammock ghillie suit is its low price. The lightweight American Camper hammock I like to use costs just $6.00 and the materials used to camouflage it are free. Not only is that cost but a fraction of what I might pay for manufactured ghillie camo, but I can sleep in mine at the end of a long day.

KIDNEY WARMER

MATERIALS NEEDED:

▼

*2 air-activated chemical
handwarmer packets,
or heated stones*

▼

*Elastic bandage
or duct tape*

If you're a devoted deer hunter, then you probably know what it means to be outside in the bitter cold for hours at a time waiting for the venison to make an appearance. In the northern areas of the country, deer season usually coincides with the onset of winter and a cold, windy November day can turn an otherwise pleasant outing into a real test of endurance. Hunters who are cold and miserable can hardly expect to shoot their best when the opportunity finally presents itself, especially if they're shivering. Still, long, motionless hours in cold weather are a fact of life for the deer hunter who wants to be successful, and sometimes the ability to endure those long hours in relative comfort is the difference between success and failure. Proper clothing and footwear are an absolute must, but it also pays to exploit other advantages, like the kidney warmer.

I've been unable to determine just where the concept of the kidney warmer originated, but it appears to be in widespread use among military snipers trained to wait hours, or even days, lying motionless in cold weather. And it works equally well for deer hunters who do the same. The idea is based on the fact that all the body's blood passes through the renal arteries about every four minutes. By applying a steady source of heat over each kidney, the blood passing through them is heated and warmth is retained in this particularly critical area.

In its most basic form, the kidney warmer consists of an ordinary elastic bandage, like those used for wrapping sprained joints, and two air-activated chemical handwarmer packets. The handwarmer packets can produce an average heat of 150 degrees Fahrenheit for up to 12 hours, depending on size, while the elastic bandage functions to hold them securely in place for the duration. An alternate and equally effective method is to fix the handwarmers in place by simply taping them to your shirt with duct tape. Just bear in mind that these wonders of modern technology can generate enough heat to produce first-degree burns on bare skin; the kidney warmer should always be worn over at least one layer of insulating material.

The kidney warmer can be held in place with duct tape or an elastic bandage—each is equally effective. However, one of my more industrious cold-weather companions has taken the idea a step further. His kidney warmer belt, made from a stout piece of three-inch-wide elastic with mating Velcro fasteners on either end, has two cloth pouches sewn to it. The position of either pouch can be adjusted by sliding it along the length of the belt and each of them has a Velcro closure flap. The beauty of his design is its versatility: The pouches will accept chemical-, charcoal-, or naphtha-type handwarmers. And if the handwarmer fuel should run out, two fist-sized stones can be heated next to the campfire or wood stove, wrapped in cloth, and used in place of commercial handwarmers to provide three or four hours of warmth.

An excellent variation on the kidney warmer, one that became possible with the invention of soft chemical handwarmer packets, is to wrap two packets lengthwise in a scarf or muffler before winding it around your neck. The packets should be positioned on either side of the neck, one over the carotid artery and one over the jugular vein, and held in place by tucking the ends of the scarf inside your jacket. Like the kidney warmer, this method effectively heats your blood as it circulates and can be used in combination with the kidney warmer for long periods of motionlessness in very cold weather.

The kidney warmer uses two chemical handwarmer packets, each held in place over a kidney with an elastic bandage, to heat the wearer's blood and increase the time he or she can comfortably stay afield in cold weather.

Still another twist on the same theme is to lay an activated handwarmer packet over your shirt sleeve on the inside of each wrist and then secure it in place with an elastic wrist brace. Applying heat directly to the blood vessels leading to and from the hands really helps to prevent cold fingers—a big plus for both rifle and bowhunters—but I personally find these "wrist warmers" uncomfortable to wear.

And those folks who always seem to suffer from cold toes while sitting in their deer blinds can also use handwarmer packets to remedy that discomfort by opening the fronts of their pac boots and sliding one packet down into the toe area of each, between the liner and the outer shell. This technique requires the roomy toe box of a pac boot to work and it can't be used with tighter-fitting insulated "hunting" boots. But if the air temperature is below freezing I recommend wearing a good, comfortable pac boot like the Sorel Dominator or LaCrosse's Expedition anyway, because my experience has been that anything less just doesn't cut it.

On the strictly practical side, being cold does nothing to enhance your mental or physical abilities, especially while you are hunting. A fit of shivering can make accurate shot placement impossible, as can a numb trigger finger, and joints that have become stiff from cold are definitely counterproductive to stealthy movement. Probably the worst way to top off a miserably cold day of hunting is to miss what should have been an easy shot (yes, that is the voice of experience). Sometimes the difference between success and failure is just a matter of degrees.

THE LOST ART OF TRACKING

If we were to believe what Hollywood's thrill-makers create for our entertainment, trackers would all be mystical, shamanlike individuals who could trail man or beast as if by magic. The truth is that any skilled tracker is just someone who has spent the time necessary to interpret minute clues that would likely be overlooked by folks who no longer need such skills to survive. And because most of us are required to make our living in the modern world, few hunters can garner the experience needed to accurately read sign. As a result, too many wounded game animals escape, especially whitetails.

Patience is the first rule of tracking. Everything that touches the earth leaves a mark, perhaps not on every place it touches, but on enough to form a trail. It falls to the tracker to find these marks, put them together, and follow them. A wounded animal will always head for safety, which in the case of deer and most other animals almost always means heading for heavy cover. It's not unusual for even a really good tracker to lose the trail in such terrain, not because the trail ended but because the animal passed over a section of ground on which its tracks became hard to distinguish. This is the point at which too many would-be trackers call it a day.

Seasoned trackers aren't so easily discouraged. They know that only rarely does an animal leave a clear trail of easily followed prints. Normal changes in terrain sometimes guarantee that the animal's tracks will eventually peter out. Experienced trackers follow sign, not just tracks. Sign, or "spoor," is any mark left by an animal's passing. Veteran trackers, like veteran car-buyers, know how to recognize and interpret a wide range of subtle indicators that would likely be overlooked by the novice.

To further illustrate, let's use a scenario typical to whitetailed deer hunting: A hunter has positioned himself in the tree line bordering a cornfield. On the other side of the cornfield is thick cedar swamp. There's a trophy buck in there that he's been watching all year.

At 7:30 A.M. the buck makes an appearance. The range is 200 yards. Our hunter takes careful aim, trying to compensate for a stiff November crosswind, and fires. The buck convulses as the bullet strikes it well behind the shoulder, but then the adrenaline kicks in and the animal hightails it toward the safety of the swamp.

Cussing his shooting, the wind, and all the swamps that ever grew, the hunter follows his prey. He picks up the trail at the spot where the buck was hit. A short search reveals hair and a few spatters of blood on a cornstalk. The dirt in the cornfield is covered with the tracks of many deer, but he has little trouble picking out those of his buck because fresh dirt has been kicked up behind them.

At the edge of the cornfield, between it and the swamp, lies an expanse of tall grass about one hundred yards wide. There are no recognizable tracks here, but the buck has left a trail like a furrow, marked on either side by walls of dewy, slanted blades that were pushed aside by the animal's passing. There's no blood trail to follow, but our hunter can see where his deer's hooves have crushed the wet plants underfoot.

At the entrance of the swamp, our hunter notices that the rough bark covering one of the cedars has been scraped by the buck's shoulder as the animal staggered between the trees. Caught in the bark are a few hairs. The ground underfoot is covered with thick sphagnum moss that will hold the imprint of a hoof for hours. The problem now is that an awful lot of deer have traversed this swamp in the last few hours, and every one of them has left a set of tracks. The hunter loses the trail after just a few yards.

But our hunter is an experienced tracker. He walks back to where he found the last track, careful not to step on any prints that might belong to his buck, and kneels down to have a closer look. He carefully examines the last set of tracks, and notices that the hindprints are close together and in line with one another. The hindprints are pressed deeply into the moss and a bit of dirt has been kicked up behind them. The left hindprint is deeper on the outside than the inside, and the moss has been twisted beneath it in a counterclockwise direction. The foreprints are both only lightly imprinted.

From these fragments of information, our hunter concludes that the buck changed its direction abruptly, jumping to the left. He finds the trail again on the other side of a large fallen log. Both front hooves have skidded over the slippery surface of the moss, plowing a couple of inches under it before stopping. The back hooves have also skidded over the moss, but haven't plowed under. The imprints of the buck's rump can be seen on either side of the tracks. The buck is apparently weakening fast, despite the lack of a steady blood trail. That can only mean that the bleeding is mostly internal.

The trail begins to meander almost aimlessly now. The hoof-prints are occasionally splayed wide apart and plow sidewise into the moss. A live cedar branch hangs limply on the side of a tree where the buck fell heavily against it. The blood trail becomes more obvious now and contains gritty material from the animal's stomach contents.

Our hunter follows the buck's spoor into an area of tall sawgrass. The sawgrass is crisscrossed with recent trails from other deer. The hunter stops to sniff the air, testing it with his poorly equipped human nose for the strong odor of bowel. Soon he detects the unmistakable odor of excrement. From there he follows his nose to the place where the buck finally fell in a thick stand of young birch.

Of course, this is just one of many possible scenarios, put together from some of my own experiences. The hunter in this example knew what he was looking for, and he didn't give up simply because the trail disappeared.

Knowing what to look for is vital to everyone who wants to become a tracker. Like detectives, appliance repairmen, or auto mechanics, trackers are simply trained observers operating in an environment with which they're familiar. They're well read when it comes to the animals they hunt; they know the animals' habits, habitat, capabilities, and anatomies. And perhaps most importantly, they don't give up when the tracks disappear.

HUNTING SCENT DISPERSERS

MATERIALS NEEDED:

▼

Film canister or pill bottle with cap

▼

Cotton

▼

Hunting scents (already prepared)

▼

Cellophane tape

▼

Electrical tape, several feet

If you're a deer hunter then you probably know at least something about commercial hunting scents marketed to help hunters attract game and to mask their own spoor. Despite recent litigation between Buck Stop, Inc., the world's leading producer of hunting scents, and the now-bankrupt ex-host of a defunct outdoor television series, probably most deer hunters (myself included) remain convinced that bottled scents increase the probability of bringing home fresh venison. But as with most every other product, the effectiveness of hunting scents is largely determined by how much homework the user does and how well he or she applies that knowledge.

By definition, scents are intended to work on a white-tailed deer's extremely sensitive olfactory system, which can detect very minute odors far below the threshold of our own comparatively dull sense of smell. It follows then that the more scent you can get into the air, the better your chances of drawing a deer within shooting range. The usual procedure is to apply several drops of scent to branches and tree trunks as high up as you can reach, which works very well for getting the smell airborne but has an effective life of one to four hours, depending on weather conditions.

A simple way to get more scent into the breeze and at the same time increase its useful duration considerably is to concentrate several ounces of it in one place and then allow only the desired amount to escape. The principle behind this time-release scent disperser can be illustrated by using plain water:

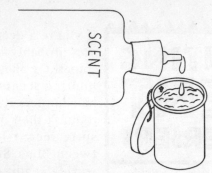

Increase the intensity and duration of any hunting scent by stuffing cotton into a snap-cap film or pill bottle and saturating its fibers with your preferred scent, forming a convenient, portable package.

If a glass filled with water is spilled onto a flat surface, the water will spread itself over a large area and evaporate in much less time than will the same amount of water left standing in the glass. The former will be absorbed into the air very quickly while the latter will undergo a slower, more steady evaporation. The same applies to hunting scents applied in drop form: they may release a strong burst of attractant into the air initially, but if you don't freshen them with more scent every couple of hours you risk their becoming too weak to be effective.

The best solution I've found is to stuff an empty film, ibuprofen, or similar bottle with cotton, which is then saturated with the desired scent. With its cap snapped or screwed in place, this makeshift scent disperser can be carried in a coat pocket without fear of making a smelly mess and uncapped after you are settled in your blind. If you're the type of hunter who likes to increase your options by taking along a variety of cover, sex, and food scents, don't forget to mark the contents of each bottle clearly and waterproof the label by covering it with cellophane tape to avoid aggravation later.

To use the scent disperser, simply remove its cap and place it as high above the ground as possible. I wrap each of my own scent dispersers with about two feet of electrical tape to secure the cap to the bottle and to tape the opened bottle to a long pole when I really want to get the scent up into the breeze. Just opening the bottle appears to radiate a strong odor for about twenty-five yards, depending on the wind, which is ideal for cover scents like fox urine. For sex scents, like Buck Stop's potent "200 Proof" doe musk, the volume of scent released (and therefore evaporated) can be increased by pulling some of the cotton above the mouth of the bottle like a lamp wick.

Before using just any bottle to make a scent disperser, consider its original contents. Unlike glass, which can be made scent-free with a thorough washing, plastic has a porous nature that tends to absorb and retain traces of whatever filled it. The powerful hunting scents are almost sure to overpower any residual odors in the plastic, but I still recommend against using plastic bottles that retain even a faint smell of their original contents. Nearly all pill bottles are acceptable, but shampoo and cologne bottles should be avoided.

Like every other product in this book, the scent disperser has proved its worth in the field, and like most of them it's so easy and inexpensive to make that several can be employed at once. When I go out for whitetails I carry about a dozen dispersers in my hunting daypack, which gives me the ability to virtually flood an area with my choice of scents, or any combination of scents. There's no guarantee that using scents (or any other product) will result in venison steak for dinner, but I've taken enough deer while using these scent dispersers to be convinced that they belong in my arsenal of hunting tools.

STRING RANGEFINDER

Since every hunting weapon in use today shoots its projectile with a curved, rainbow-like trajectory, accurate range estimation is critical to hunting success. This is especially true when shooting high-trajectory, short-range weapons like bows and crossbows. Knowing how high or low from zero an arrow, bolt, or bullet will impact at any given range is a matter of knowing your weapon and practicing consistent shooting techniques. But determining the distance from shooter to target is one of the toughest marksmanship skills to master no matter what your weapon, particularly in conditions of low light or heavy shadow. And if you can't accurately estimate the range to your target, you can't accurately calculate where your projectile will impact, which often results in a miss or a wounded animal instead of a clean kill.

Once again modern technology has entered the arena with a variety of optical rangefinding devices, most notably those sold by the Crosman company under its "Ranging" label. Unfortunately, manufactured rangefinders represent a sometimes considerable outlay of cash for archers who have already spent too much money on pin sights, release devices, and other required accessories. But the optical rangefinder was preceded long ago by another very simple rangefinding tool that costs practically nothing to make, yet is simple enough for a child to use.

The basis for this rangefinder is 50 to 100 yards of nylon string, marked at 1-yard intervals with a single overhand knot. Begin by wrapping the string lengthwise around a yardstick with a series of even side-by-side wraps. When the ends of the yardstick have been completely covered and can hold no more wraps, hold the yardstick and string firmly together with one hand and run a permanent marker across either end to mark

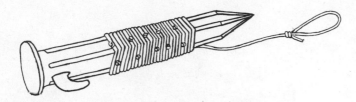

Fifty to one hundred yards of nylon string with knots tied at one-yard intervals can be wrapped around a plastic tent stake to create an accurate rangefinding device for bowhunting.

the string at one-yard increments. Then uncoil the string and, beginning at the last mark you made, repeat this procedure until the entire length of string is marked at one-yard gradations.

At this point the string rangefinder is ready for use, but only in broad daylight. Since most deer hunters arrive at their blinds or bowstands well before sunrise, the string needs to be marked tactilely as well as visually to enable distances to be measured by feel. The best way to do that is to tie a simple overhand knot at each one-yard mark, thus enabling you to measure elapsed yardage by counting the number of knots that slide between your fingers. It's true that tying knots in the string does shorten it, but the average loss over 100 yards (that is, 100 knots) is under 10 inches, not enough to make a difference either way.

To make this yardage measure even more functional in the field, I recommend tying one end around a plastic tent stake with a slipknot. The tent stake provides a pocket-sized, tangle-free means of wrapping the knotted line and it can be shoved into the ground to serve as an anchor for making distance measurements in open spaces. Otherwise, the free end of the string can be looped over or tied to a convenient branch and the wraps reeled off as you walk backward toward your blind, counting knots as you go.

Of course, it's also true that white-tailed deer can be completely unpredictable—which is precisely why we call it hunting. You can measure the distance from blind to bait pile or scrape, calculate exactly where your shot will impact at that

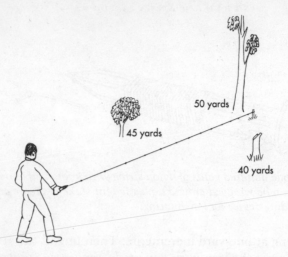

50 yards

45 yards

40 yards

Using the string rangefinder: anchor one end to the point being measured and walk backward to your blind, counting off knots as they pass between your fingers. Unlike costly optical rangefinders, the string rangefinder can be used in complete darkness.

range, and figure out just how much compensation you'll need to allow to make a clean, one-shot kill, only to have that trophy buck walk by at a spot you never expected. For that reason, it's a good idea for archers to range at least one prominent terrain feature in every direction they might possibly have to shoot. Distances to stumps, downed trees, and other easily distinguishable landmarks can be scribbled onto a rough map for quick reference. Such a map is well worth the trouble it takes to draw. Even if your deer takes an unexpected route, it's almost always easier to estimate its range when you have a known distance to which you can refer. For example, it's simpler and more precise to guess that a deer is 10 yards on the other side of a stump that you know is exactly 30 yards distant than it is to guess the entire distance without predetermined reference points.

One obvious problem with using the string rangefinder is that it can't tell you the distance to anything unless you first measure, so it isn't likely to find favor with stillhunters or long-range riflemen. But if you're a bowhunter or muzzleloader hunting from a fixed blind or bowstand, this simple device could allow you to take the money you were going to spend on a commercial rangefinder and invest it in other equipment.

DISPATCHING WOUNDED GAME

Not much has been written about field techniques used to dispatch wounded animals swiftly and humanely, and for good reason. While many of us are born with an instinctive, primeval desire to hunt, each of us, with rare exceptions, also possesses a God-given human reluctance to kill. It's one thing to take an animal's life quickly from afar with a high-power rifle, but quite another to end its life personally, up close, with your own two hands. Although one-shot kills are always the goal of any respectable hunter, sometimes a hunter only wounds the animal with the first shot—and shooting again might not be desirable for the hunter who wants to preserve the head, neck, and meat of a trophy. For most folks who seriously injure deer with their automobiles, shooting isn't even an option, which often leaves them in the unenviable position of either watching the animal slowly die or taking matters into their own hands and finishing the process with whatever weapons are available. An animal's slow and painful death is a terrible thing for both the animal itself and its witness; a good many people have given themselves nightmares by their own well-intentioned yet clumsy attempts at euthanasia.

There are two humane methods of dispatching wounded game, both fast and relatively painless. The first method is especially effective on deer that still have enough fight left to cause harm with hooves or antlers, both of which are potentially vicious natural weapons. (I know of at least two people who were killed when road-struck deer rolled over the downswept front end of their late-model cars, through the windshield, and into the front seat, still kicking and fighting wildly.) The trick is to avoid injury to yourself by pinning the animal in a position that allows a swift final stroke to be administered. Rodeo cowboys know that lying across the neck of even a large hoofed animal will make it impossible for that animal to raise its head, and therefore unable to rise to its feet. Grabbing an injured white-tailed deer by the antlers or ears and forcing it to the ground under your body weight will immobilize the animal long enough for you to end its life with one swift stroke.

In this method that single, merciful stroke is delivered by a long-bladed stabbing instrument with a sharp point. For me, that has usually been a knife, but I've used a screwdriver in a pinch with equal success. With the animal's neck pinned firmly against the ground, cup your lower hand under its chin and pull its head back to expose the underside of the chin. Then, with your opposite hand, drive the knife hard into the soft lower palate, through the upper palate, and into the deer's brain. I've used this technique many, many times, and in every case the deer has simply shuddered once and gone limp, dead instantly. Just make certain the blade you use is long enough to get the job done. The five-inch blade of the USAF survival knife is too short for this method, but the M-7 bayonet (six and one-half inches) or Buck's "General" bowie knife (seven and one-half inches) are very effective.

A second, equally effective method that works well with shorter, narrow blades involves stabbing into an animal's brain through its ear. Every animal that has ears also has an opening in its skull beneath each of them to allow the passage of processed sound waves into the brain. As many poachers know, this soft spot also permits a small-caliber bullet to penetrate into the brain unimpeded, causing immediate death. The same result can be obtained by taking firm hold of a deer's large ear and driving a blade through that opening.

The cleanest, most efficient method of dispatching any wounded animal mercifully is to drive a hunting knife into its brain. This method is also useful for trophy hunters who want to preserve the head and as much of their prey's meat as possible.

In describing both of these techniques I've used the white-tailed deer as an example, but the same soft spots exist on nearly every animal of every species. What's hardest about applying them in the field or on the highway is overcoming our natural aversion to killing sufficiently to deliver that one forceful thrust. If you find that you're one of the many who just can't do it, don't feel as if you've failed as a hunter. Every primitive culture, from the African Bushmen to the Miskito tribe of South America, has regarded euthanasia—which is a part of daily life when hunting with primitive weapons—as a solemn and spiritual experience. Hunters who must sometimes kill their prey with their own hands develop a greater appreciation for life in general and a greater respect for the animals they hunt.

MEAT AND FISH SMOKERS

MATERIALS NEEDED:

▼

Parachute cord or string

▼

10–12 eight-foot poles

▼

Campfire, with lots of hot coals

▼

Sticks, leaves, sod

In the days before canning and refrigeration had become necessary parts of life, the edible life of perishable foods was extended by drying. In hot, sunny weather, that usually meant just hanging finely sliced strips of meat, fish, or fruit in the open air to dehydrate naturally. If the weather was too cool or humid for sun drying, another source of dry heat had to be employed, which most often meant that the food was parched in a smoker. Fresh meat—especially fish—decays quickly in its natural state because most bacteria require moisture for their decomposition work. Driving the moisture out of meat could extend its edible life several hundred times, which meant that hunters and travelers could venture much farther without the need to constantly resupply. An added bonus was that removing the water from trail food reduced its weight by about seventy-five percent, an advantage backpackers still appreciate today.

But smoking had an advantage over sun drying: it gave meat and fish a tangy taste that was welcomed in those days when salt was prized for its scarcity and most spices were picked from the wild. The distinctly pleasant flavor left by drying meat in warm, smoky air made bland trail fare, which was frequently unsalted, more palatable. The flavor was actually just a by-product of the drying process, but it became so popular that smoking continued even when it was no longer necessary for preserving food. Unfortunately, most of the commercially sold smoked fish and meat I've tried have been inferior to those that are smoked at home.

In a genuine survival situation where the most important

goals are to reduce food's weight and increase its edible life, meat (including poultry) and fish can be prepared for smoking by simply cutting them into thin strips, washing them if possible, and drying them as is. But if you're smoking in the backyard, meat strips can be salted and seasoned with garlic, onion powder, and black pepper to create delicious kippered steaks or jerky. For all types of fish, leave the skin and scales in place and split the cleaned fish lengthwise at the spine to form two long slabs. Slice these slabs into narrow sections and pickle them for 12 hours in a brine made from a quarter cup kosher salt per gallon of water, a tablespoon of lemon juice concentrate per gallon of water, and a half cup of brown sugar per five gallons of water. Some folks prefer to substitute honey for brown sugar in this recipe, but, either way, an overnight soak in this modest brine solution will result in some of the best smoked fish you've ever tasted.

The simplest type of smoker consists of nothing more than a small, smoky campfire over which thinly sliced strips of meat or fish are hung from a spit suspended by two forked poles. The first step in using this or any type of smoker is to build a hot bed of live coals by burning dry wood, and then cover those coals with lengths of green wood. Suitable woods include maple, oak, hickory, mesquite, apple, and cherry; pine and cedar should be avoided because they impart a distinctly unpleasant flavor to the finished product. Since the goal isn't to roast the meat but to thoroughly dehydrate it, there should be no flames and the fire should never become too hot to place your bare hand between it and the meat.

The drawback to smoking over an open fire is that it takes too long. Smoke and warmed air generated by the smoldering green wood are deflected away from drying food by the merest breeze, extending the required drying time to as much as a full day. Fabricated smokers cut that time in half by containing the warm smoke in a ventilated expansion chamber that allows a constant, even flow of moisture to the outside and thoroughly permeates the meat with smoke flavor.

Probably the easiest type of fabricated smoker is the tepee smoker. It consists of a tepee frame made from 10 to 12 eight-

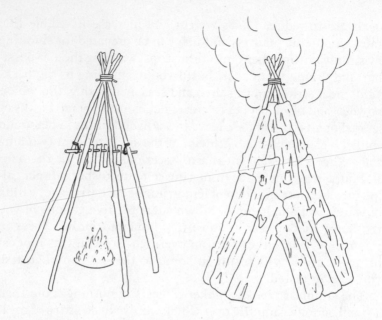

The purpose of any smoker is to thoroughly dry the flesh being smoked, as this tepee-type smoker shown here will do.

foot poles (dead wood is okay) tied together at their narrow ends and then spread out from a vertical position to form a wigwam-type frame. Loops of parachute cord or string tied onto either side of the frame about halfway up its length can be used to suspend a wooden spit onto which the meat strips have been speared, or you can simply thread the strips onto a length of cord tied off on either side of the frame.

Next, a small fire is lit inside the frame and allowed to burn down to hot coals. The live coals are then covered with sections of green wood taken from newly fallen trees. If the coals are hot enough, these green sections will begin to smolder quickly, producing copious amounts of thick smoke. If that doesn't happen, remove the green wood and lay down a bed of dried wood—preferably of the same kind—leaving about an inch of air space between pieces, and cover it with the green wood. This will allow the coals to feed on easily burned material while producing enough heat to make the green wood above them smolder vigorously.

Finally, cover the outside of the frame with more poles, followed by sticks, leaves, sod, and other available materials. My own preference is to use slabs broken from the outside of rotting stumps or logs because these are readily available in most wooded areas and a large area of the frame can be covered by each piece, saving both time and effort. Your goal isn't to seal the outside of the frame completely, but to impede the rising smoke just enough to cause it to swirl around a bit, flavoring every piece of drying meat evenly before escaping to the outside. After the outside surface of the tepee smoker is covered—except for a small triangular opening through which to feed the fire with air and wood—smoke should still seep freely through, taking evaporated moisture with it.

The tepee smoker can be made to work as well as any other type, but I'd be remiss in my responsibility to the reader if I didn't include a warning: the tepee smoker is, by virtue of the materials used in its construction, often quite flammable. If the only material available to cover the frame and seal in the smoke is dried vegetation (leaves and ferns, for example) it's a good idea to thoroughly saturate that flammable material with water before laying it over the frame. Also, make certain that the frame legs are spread as far apart as possible and that the fire is small and located in the center of the frame. As further protection, I also like to place the fire in an excavated pit or surround it with stones to help contain popping coals. Use of the tepee smoker dates back to before the arrival of Europeans in the New World, and the possibility of its catching fire is pretty remote, but it always pays to think ahead and exercise caution. And, of course, be sure you put your fire completely out when you're done.

A second, even more efficient type of field-expedient smoker is an excavated version I call the dugout smoker. It consists of an open-top hole—essentially a squared notch—dug into the side of a dirt hill. In this instance, the drying rack is made by spearing the meat strips over a long branch and shoving one end of that branch firmly into the soil of the smoker's back wall, suspending it and the food it holds horizontally over the smoking fire. The fire is laid in a pit dug into the bottom of the dugout and is identical to the fire used in the tepee smoker and every other type of smoker.

When the fire is ready and the meat hung for drying, cover the front and top of the dugout smoker with branches and sections of wood, leaving a small triangular opening at the front through which to tend the fire. Again, the goal isn't to seal in the smoke completely, but to impede its escape just enough for it to swirl around the meat strips, drying them evenly and saturating each piece with smoky flavor.

All three of the smokers described here are meant for use in the field, but suburban and rural dwellers with a fresh deer or a large catch of fish will probably opt for a smoker made from an old refrigerator, or even a 55-gallon drum, with welded wire grates for drying racks. There are innumerable methods by which to construct a smoker from the materials at hand, but the procedure and the objective are always the same with any of them. If your smoker will dry meat into jerky and smoke fish in about twelve hours, then it's a good one.

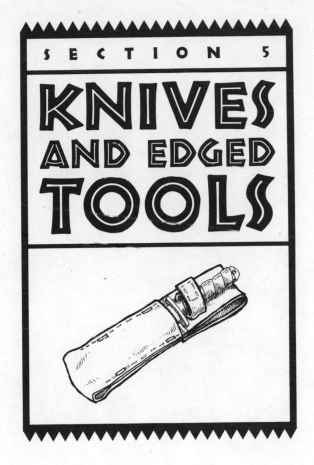

SECTION 5

KNIVES AND EDGED TOOLS

PRACTICAL KNIFE AND TOOL SHARPENING

There was once a time when the ability to sharpen knives and other edged tools was as vital to daily life as the ability to notch fence rails and butcher your own meat. The frontiersman's knife and hatchet were as close to being multifunctional tools as anything made before the latter half of this century, and since sharpness was the reason to have those tools, necessity dictated that their owners be skilled at keeping a keen edge on them. But nowadays sharp tools—especially knives—have become pretty rare, probably because a keen blade isn't as necessary to survival as it once was. As a result, knife sharpening has become almost a forgotten skill.

I've passed along my own sharpening techniques to a number of friends and I've concluded that the easiest way to teach most anyone to sharpen a knife is to first explain what a cutting edge is, how it looks, and what causes it to be sharp or dull. As with any skill, mastery is achieved only through long practice, but it's a lot easier for a beginner to create a sharp edge when he or she knows what one looks like.

To begin with, there are two edges on any blade. First is the ground edge, which was put on when the blade was shaped at the factory. There are five basic types of ground edges, listed here in order of sharpness: hollow ground, semi-hollow ground, flat ground, sabre ground, and diamond ground.

The hollow ground edge is formed by cutting a wide groove into each side of the blade. The radius of this groove extends from the spine (top) of the blade down to the cutting edge, creating a very narrow, very keen point that sharpens easily and holds its edge. Its one drawback is that removing the amount of material required to form it makes a blade too thin and fragile for use on a field or kitchen knife. For that reason the hollow ground edge is usually limited to use on straightrazors.

The semi-hollow ground edge is an abbreviated version of the hollow ground edge that can be found on probably most hunting knives made today. It also features a groove cut into the length of its blade along each side, but in this case the groove radius extends from the center of the blade down to the cutting edge. This design is very popular because it leaves about half the blade at full thickness and strength while providing nearly the sharpness of a hollow ground edge.

The flat ground edge is commonly used on pocketknives because their blades are too thin to accept a groove cut into both sides, but sometimes it can be found on large blades, like Cold Steel's rugged Trailmaster Bowie. Considered by many to be the ideal woodsman's edge, the flat ground edge gets its name from the wide, flat bevels on each side of the blade, beginning at the spine and terminating at the cutting edge. Seen in cross section, the blade appears as an elongated wedge. The flat ground edge sharpens quickly, holds its edge well, and stands up to hacking and chopping better than thinner semi-hollow ground edges.

The sabre ground edge is found mostly on military knives like the beefy USAF Survival Knife and Imperial Schrade's M-7S survival knife. It consists of a flat ground edge that extends about halfway up the blade, a configuration that leaves as much strength in the blade as possible while still providing a ground edge that can be honed to shaving sharpness. Relative to the three edge types already mentioned, sabre ground knives dull more quickly, but the tradeoff is that they can withstand brutal abuse from prying and hacking.

Last is the diamond ground edge, so called because the blade appears diamond-shaped when seen end-on. This design is of course limited to double-edged knives and daggers. Originally intended as a stabbing weapon rather than a cutting tool, the dagger is hard to sharpen—you'll see why shortly—and inherently weak because its spine is ground away to form a second cutting edge, literally taking the backbone out of the blade.

The locus at which all of these ground edges intersect is the cutting edge, or honed edge. This is the edge we're concerned with when sharpening any type of blade, but an understanding of the different types of ground edges is important because the type of ground edge ultimately determines how sharp the cutting edge can be made. To illustrate, if two blades of equal width and thickness are given sabre and flat ground edges, respectively, and then viewed end-on, you'll see that the more expansive flat ground edge comes to a much sharper point at the cutting edge. And it will be equally obvious why the sabre ground edge is the strongest design of all. Generally speaking, the narrower the V formed by the ground edge, the sharper the cutting edge will be, and the wider the V, the stronger the blade.

To get the cutting edge sharp, it must be brought to a sharp point from both sides and then polished to remove microscopic burrs. A blade becomes dull when the sharp point formed by its cutting edge becomes rounded and worn from wear. Sharpening it requires only that it be brought back to a sharp point by wearing down both sides of the cutting edge equally with a honing stone.

The first step is to apply what I call a "primary edge," a rough cutting edge that can later be polished to razor sharpness. The angle of the primary edge also has a lot to do with how sharp a blade can be made. Once again, the steeper the V formed by it, the sharper the final edge will be. I've purposely reshaped the factory cutting edge on every knife I own so that the edges form a narrower V with longer sides and a keener point. I prefer a large, coarse carborundum stone for this operation, although in really severe cases of dullness I sometimes employ a sharp diamond-cut file first. I never recommend using any type of electric grinder as these will actually destroy whatever cutting edge the blade already has, and one slip can ruin the looks of your favorite knife forever.

Remember, applying the primary cutting edge requires only that you wear away just enough metal from each side to bevel it to a sharp point. Most authorities recommend that you do this by grinding the blade against the stone with a circular motion while simultaneously drawing it slowly back, from handle to tip. Most also specify an angle at which you should hold the blade relative to the surface of the stone. But the real issue is bringing the cutting edge to a sharp point by grinding nice, even bevels along the length of the blade on both sides, and if you accomplish that, you did it right, whatever the angle.

During preliminary sharpening with a caborundum stone it helps to keep the stone's surface wet with water and free of residue while honing. Water helps the stone abrade more efficiently by washing away metal and stone particles that accumulate between the blade and its surface. Carborundum stones may also be used dry, although this is not as effective, but you should never, ever put any kind of oil on a carborundum stone. Oil penetrates deeply into the stone's coarse pores and combines with the dust created during honing to form a hard, nonabrasive glaze that completely ruins the stone. The finished primary edge should be keen enough to catch against your thumb when you run it lightly across (never along) the blade from either side.

The next step is to smooth and polish the rough primary edge with a finer, harder abrasive. That would be an "Arkansas oilstone," so called because its composition is such that it sharpens (polishes) better when light oil is applied to its surface. It's best to start with a medium-grade oilstone and just a few drops of oil, and you might want to keep a rag handy for wiping off honing residue. Work both sides of the blade against (not away from) the oiled surface of the stone with a circular motion that covers the full length of the blade, from handle to tip.

Again, there is no absolutely mandatory angle at which you should hold the knife relative to the honing surface—you'll have to find the ideal angle. Your goal is to polish the primary cutting edge to a smooth, flat-sided triangle that terminates in a very sharp point along the length of the blade on both sides. Doing that requires that you work the primary edge flush against the stone, at whatever angle, to make the sides of the cutting-edge V as flat and straight as possible. When you find the correct angle you'll be able to see it and you'll feel a definite drag against the blade. If you don't feel this drag as you rotate the blade against the stone, either you've shifted your honing angle, or the blade's primary edge is not flat but rounded outward; either case is contrary to your purpose. And bear in mind that keeping the cutting edge flat against the

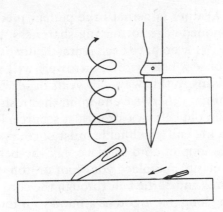

Knife and tool sharpening is almost a lost art, but if you first understand what a sharp edge is, applying it to your tools becomes much easier.

stone while honing the radius near a knife's tip requires an increase in the angle between blade and stone.

A loss of friction might also mean your stone is clogged. After several dozen strokes you'll observe that a hard glaze of metal particles, stone dust, and coagulated oil has formed over the surface of your whetstone, reducing its abrasiveness. The particles that form this glaze can be put into suspension and wiped off by adding more oil as you work and then wiping the stone clean with a rag when you've finished with it.

After you've made the edge as sharp as you can with the medium oilstone, it's time to switch to a fine oilstone to give the edge a final polishing. The procedure is exactly the same as that used with the medium stone, except in this instance you should end up with an edge that will shave the hair off your forearm. (I don't recommend you test the sharpness of a blade in that manner, however, because as your skill improves you'll soon have a bald forearm.) A more acceptable way to see if a blade is truly sharp is to scrape it against your thumbnail. If it catches against the nail easily with just light pressure, the edge is capable of butchering a deer.

The final step in my own sharpening process is to strop the cutting edge to hair-splitting sharpness with an old leather belt, in much the same way a barber freshens the edge on his straightrazor. Leather is perhaps the perfect medium for polishing a well-honed edge to shaving sharpness, but the commercial strops I've seen have been fantastically overpriced. An old leather trousers belt, while narrower, will work just as well, and recycling in this way adds years of serviceable life to an item that might otherwise end up in the trash.

To convert an old belt to a strop, just secure a loop of heavy cord to the buckle end (the buckle must of course be removed first). With the loop of cord in place, lay the belt flat on the floor, rough side up, and place your foot on top of the buckle end. Pass the free end of the belt through the cord loop to form another, sliding loop that tightens around your foot, anchoring the belt. From a seated position, use your opposite hand to bend the free end across your opposite knee and hold it there. Extending your anchored foot will result in a taut, flat leather surface that's nearly ideal for "standing-up" the honed edge of most everything from a hatchet to a paring knife.

To use a strop, stroke the blade in the opposite direction of that used during honing: *with* the edge instead of against it. This puts a fine polish on the cutting edge and smooths microscopic burrs outward to form an extremely sharp point. For best results, use the technique employed by barbers, stroking each side of the cutting edge alternately against the leather an equal number of times. In the end you should have an edge that can shave strips from a sheet of notebook paper without snagging—although if you're a beginner that isn't likely to happen on the first several attempts.

Sharpening the cutting edge of any tool is an easy skill to develop once you have the proper tools and an idea of what needs to be done. The most important thing is to understand what makes a blade sharp. The rest will come with practice.

NONSLIP CUTTING TOOL HANDLES

MATERIALS NEEDED:

▼

1 roll Guard-Tex safety tape

▼

24-hour clear epoxy resin and hardener

No one would dispute that using a sharpened, hand-held cutting tool with a slippery handle is dangerous, especially for its user. Yet a good many belt knives, hatchets, axes, and machetes come from the factory with handles that are very hard to hang onto under commonly encountered field conditions. Chopping wood in the rain with a slick-handled ax is just looking for trouble, while animal fat and blood can give knife handles all the grip of wet bar soap. If you're buying a new tool, modern textured and rubberized handles help to alleviate the problem, but that doesn't do anything for the slippery-handled tools you might already own.

I found an effective and inexpensive solution to this problem about ten years ago. I'd been wrapping the handles of my axes and slippery-handled knives with safety tape, a marvelous, multipurpose product of technology made from surgical-grade gauze impregnated with natural latex. Available in a variety of colors and widths, the stuff adheres tenaciously to itself and nothing else. When wrapped around the handle of most any tool, it provides a clean but sticky grip and cushions against the shock of hacking and chopping. The trouble was that it tended to unravel after awhile when used on tools that got heavy use, like shovels and axes. It needed to be more durable.

After a number of more or less unsuccessful experiments, I tried saturating the wrapped handle of my Buck Pathfinder—a very sharp and notoriously slippery-handled knife—with 2-ton, or 24-hour, epoxy resin. A day later, when the resin had cured, the result was just what I'd been hoping for. The combination of safety tape and epoxy had formed a hard yet pliable shell that

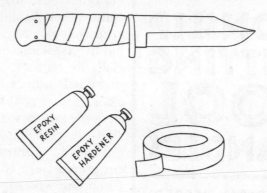

A slippery-handled knife or ax is dangerous to its user. Create effective and durable nonslip handle coverings with safety tape and epoxy.

gave the handle a cushiony feel and a surface texture similar to that of 50-grit sandpaper.

When buying epoxy for this project, make certain to get the 24-hour type, not the quick-setting type. Quick-setting epoxy is a very good adhesive, but it dissolves when exposed to water and other liquids for a long period of time, making the handle slimy and defeating the purpose of covering it in the first place.

To begin, wrap several snug turns of safety tape around one end of the handle. You'll need to hold the end of the tape in place with a thumb for the first couple of turns because it won't stick to the handle, only to itself. After that, friction will prevent it from sliding around the handle. Cover the desired length with overlapping diagonal wraps from one end to the other and back again, until you've applied four or five layers. Next, smear a liberal layer of mixed epoxy resin over the tape and work it into the fabric with a finger. When the safety tape is saturated, stand the tool in a corner and let the covering harden. That's basically all there is to it.

Of course, I have developed a few variations on this technique that make it a bit more versatile. One of them is to sprinkle fine, beach-type sand over the coated handle before the epoxy sets completely and follow that with a light coat of spray paint—the latter being just for looks. The cured handle will have a very rough, abrasive grip that's easy to hang onto even when covered with fish slime or venison fat. And because the paint was sprayed on while the epoxy was still setting, the finished handle will hold its color indefinitely without chipping or peeling.

I've also used this method to completely replace handles on full-tang knives (the tang is the portion of the blade that extends into the handle). There are quite a few fine old age-hardened blades out there whose washer-type leather handles have dry-rotted to the point of becoming useless, and many newer knives whose handles have broken, mainly from being thrown at hard objects. So long as the blade has a full-length tang to build on, the handle can be remade using safety tape and epoxy, without removing either the buttcap or the fingerguard.

To make a new knife handle, first cover the tang with a light coat of epoxy mixture to ensure that the hardened fabric of the safety tape can never come loose from it. Follow that with about a dozen wraps of safety tape at either end of the tang, snug against the buttcap and fingerguard. After that simply fill in the blank spots with wrapped safety tape until you've achieved the desired thickness and configuration. You can create a nice grooved pattern like that used on military knives by alternating wraps of, say, one-inch safety tape with half-inch, or you can shape the hardened handle later with a belt or wheel grinder. If you choose to do the latter, I suggest applying a coat of epoxy after every six wraps and finishing the shaped handle with a final coat of epoxy.

You can also use this process to wrap the wooden handles of axes and hatchets with a dozen or so hardened layers just below the head. As probably most of us know, this is the area of the handle most likely to be splintered or broken by a missed swing. By protecting the first six or eight inches below the head, you can prolong the life of a wooden ax handle considerably: damaged wraps of tape are much easier to replace than a broken handle.

As for durability, all I can tell you is that I've yet to wear out a wrapped or replacement handle made with this technique, despite years of use under sometimes brutal conditions. Both

wrapped and replacement tool handles become virtually indestructible in the field, although you should bear in mind that
harsh solvents, including those used to clean firearms, may dis-
solve the epoxy to some degree. The tape-and-epoxy covering is
inexpensive, but best of all, it can go a long way toward preventing serious injuries in the wild, where professional medical
attention might not be possible.

If you'd like to give this nonslip handle covering a try, a free
sample roll of safety tape can be obtained by writing to: General Bandages, 8300 LeHigh Avenue, Morton Grove, Illinois
60053-0909; telephone (708) 966-8383. You won't be given a
choice about the width or color of your sample roll, but if you
decide to order more, safety tape is available in white, blue,
green, and flesh colors, and in standard widths of one-half to
three inches, in half-inch increments.

REPLACEMENT KNIFE SHEATH

MATERIALS NEEDED:

▼

Automobile seat-belt strapping, 2′

▼

Heavy darning needle

▼

Spool of nylon carpet thread

▼

2 mating strips of Velcro, 2″ long

▼

Epoxy or Elmer's Glue

▼

Superglue

If you're one of those unlucky individuals who owns a fixed-blade hunting or survival knife that no longer has a sheath, this project will help you get that knife back in the woods where it belongs. Some original sheaths have been cut badly by a sharp blade, a few have dry-rotted, and many have been simply lost somehow. But whatever the reason for needing a new sheath, most folks in search of a replacement to use with their favorite knife come away disappointed. Many of the few generic aftermarket sheaths I've seen don't fit the knife for which they're intended and appear to have been constructed with price rather than quality in mind.

Carrying a sharp belt knife without a sheath poses a distinct danger to its owner and is somewhat akin to using a firearm without a working safety catch. Without a sheath there's really no safe place to put the knife that still guarantees it won't be left behind.

A few creative people have made replacement sheaths for their knives from tanned leather, but heavyweight cowhide—if you can find it—is both expensive and difficult to work with. Untreated leather also tends to crack, shrink, and dry-rot. An easier and cheaper medium from which to make replacement knife sheaths is something that we all use every day: the woven nylon seat belt found in every vehicle made in the last quarter century. The strength and durability of the seat belt is beyond question: it never breaks in an accident and it always outlasts the vehicle to which it's mounted. Junkyards are filled with old cars and trucks that still have intact seat belts. The people running these junkyards seldom recognize just how useful seat-belt strapping is, because they'll sell it in quantity for next to nothing and sometimes even give it away.

With a two-foot length of seat-belt material in hand—remember, it comes in a variety of colors from which to select—the only materials you still need to construct a knife sheath are a large darning needle, a spool of carpet thread (also available in your choice of colors from arts and crafts stores, drugstores, and some supermarkets), two mating pieces of Velcro, and a tube or bottle of superglue. Some sewing is required to make a knife sheath—but only a stitch strong enough to securely fasten two pieces of material together.

The easiest way to measure the sheath to its intended blade is to use the knife itself as a gauge. Lay the knife lengthwise along the seat-belt strap and fold the strap into shape around it before you do any cutting or sewing (see illustration). Except for the retaining strap that fastens around the knife handle with Velcro (or a snap fastener, available from most arts and crafts stores), the sheath is made from a single continuous length of material.

When you have form-fitted the case to the knife, cut off the remaining seat-belt material at the belt loop end and sew the blade pouch closed along either side. Use the simple in-and-out loop, or "sine wave," stitch used on factory sheaths, except in this case you'll apply it manually instead of with a machine. Seat-belt strapping is fairly easy to get a needle through, even at double or triple thickness, but it can be made even easier by folding the strap into the desired configuration atop a softwood board and nailing it together with small finishing nails spaced every one-eighth inch. Drive the nails just far enough in to penetrate both sides of the seat-belt material. Next, pull the nails back out with a pair of pliers and use the holes left by them as a guide to stitching the sheath together.

When stitching the sheath, start with the blade pouch. Don't sew the belt loop closed until you've attached the retaining strap. Begin at either end of either side and loop the thread in one side of the material and out the other in serpentine fashion at least one-eighth inch from the outer edge. It may help to tie a large knot in the free end of the thread to keep it from pulling through as you run the first few stitches. When you've sewed the length of one side together from top to bottom, add another row of stitches from bottom to top, running alternately with the first row. The completed stitching should look like one continuous line of thread on either side.

The retaining strap, which wraps around the handle and attaches to itself to prevent the knife from falling out of its sheath, can be made from a piece of seat-belt material, but narrower-width fabric strapping works best. The length of the retaining strap of course depends upon the circumference of the knife handle: the strap should be cut about an inch longer than what is required to wrap around the handle. Based on my own experience I also recommend placing the strap as close to the fingerguard as possible to prevent the sheathed knife from exerting enough leverage on it to pull the Velcro apart. This location is almost mandatory if the sheath is to be equipped with a thigh tiedown on its bottom.

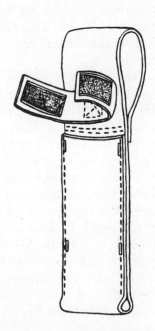

Once you've established the desired length and placement of the retaining strap, sew the mating pieces of Velcro to it using the same sine wave stitch you employed for the sides of the knife pouch. The belt loop can now be sewn closed with a double row of stitches running parallel to one another.

With the retaining strap securely fastened and the belt loop

A knife without a sheath is like a gun without a safety catch. This seat-belt sheath is inexpensive, durable, and easy to make. It will accommodate a variety of knives.

sewn closed, the sheath is finished but not quite ready for use. As any experienced backpacker can tell you, the cut, or "raw," ends of most types of fabric will unravel with use, eventually to the point where the seam's stitches have nothing left to hold onto. That and similar problems can be prevented by saturating the raw edges of the cut fabric with epoxy or Elmer's Glue in a strip about one-eighth inch wide. When the glue dries it will form a hard edge that will not only keep the threads from unraveling but also serve to stiffen the fabric around the mouth of the blade pouch and make it easier to resheath a drawn blade.

In the same vein, it's also a good idea to dribble liquid "super glue" down into the inside seams at either edge of the blade pouch to help stiffen the sheath and prevent the blade from cutting through the seams. In cases where the knife blade is narrow enough, you can install a pop-rivet on each side of the blade pouch just below the opening. You can also protect the seams from a keen edge by driving long-shank staples, like those used in staple guns, through the lines of stitching at regular intervals on each side of the sheath, and then bending the protruding ends of the staples down hard with a pair of pliers. Either way, it's still a good idea to harden the stitches with a liberal amount of "super glue"; in most cases that will be sufficient.

The beauty of the seat-belt sheath for fixed-blade knives isn't just that it's cheap and easy to make, but that it's also very functional. The flat, square-bottomed sheath will accept a variety of similar-sized knives—for instance, a sheath made for the Ka-Bar-style USMC knife will also accept the Gerber LMF and the new Buck M9 Field Knife. Perhaps even more important to the southpaws among us is the way the sheath adapts to either right- or left-hand carry; the cutting edge can face front or back depending on the wearer's preference. You'll also notice that a small tunnel was formed in the fold at the bottom of the blade pouch by the stitching along its sides. Survivalists and primitive campers who like the strength and utility of large, heavy blades can thread a length of strong cord through this tunnel to equip the sheath with a tiedown that will keep the cased blade from flopping and banging against the wearer's thigh as he or she walks. A few of my own finished sheaths have been hardened and form-fitted to a knife by saturating the material with epoxy resin and allowing it to dry for 24 hours with the petroleum jelly–covered blade inside. One of my unusually ambitious projects was a survival-knife sheath that sported two paraphernalia pockets with Velcro-closure flaps on the outside, à la the Imperial/Schrade M7-S survival knife.

So don't resign those sheathless knives to the bottom of a kitchen drawer—put them back in the field where they belong. The seat-belt sheath is durable, inexpensive, functional, and, perhaps most importantly, made from an item that currently has almost no value to anyone. It seems in keeping with the times to employ a castoff commodity, one that is not presently and possibly can never be recycled, to create a necessary piece of outdoor equipment.

If you're someone who works with your hands, it's likely you appreciate the compact strength and utility of a large folding knife. Rescue personnel carry these knives to slash through seat belts at car accidents and to cut away restrictive clothing from injured victims; working folks carry them to perform a multitude of cutting, scraping, and light prying chores on the job; outdoorsmen carry them for filleting fish and performing other jobs that require a delicate, razor-sharp touch. A large, quality folding knife like Buck's Ranger or Schrade's Bear Paw is perhaps the ideal complement to a heavy-duty survival-belt knife.

Ironically, many knife makers detract from the usefulness of their large folders by offering them without belt holsters. These knives are too large to be carried in a trouser pocket and in many cities tucking one in a pocket runs afoul of concealed weapons laws. Aftermarket generic knife holsters are available, but are frequently overpriced and of poor quality, and seldom fit the knife for which they were purchased. Fortunately, that problem is easily remedied with a little cutting and sewing.

The folding-knife holster I use (sometimes even for folders that are sold with factory holsters) is made from seat-belt or similarly wide strapping material. Nylon seat-belt strapping is durable, impervious to age and moisture, and wide enough to accommodate most large folders. Begin with at least a foot of strapping—I recommend two feet, just in case you make a mistake—laid out on a flat surface. No measuring is required to get the proper fit; just lay the closed knife on top of the strap and fold the strap back over the bolster (hinged) end until all but an inch or so of the knife handle is covered. This will be the pouch that carries your knife.

Holding the knife and strap in the same position, fold the opposite end of the strap over the portion of handle still exposed. This will be the closure flap on the finished holster. Since the flap will be held down over the cased knife by mating strips of hook-and-loop (Velcro) material, it should overlap the mouth of the knife pouch by about two inches. When you've determined the appropriate length, cut off the remainder of the strap with sharp scissors or a knife.

Next, cut a four-inch section from the remaining strap material to serve as a belt loop. With the knife still folded inside, turn the unsewn holster over and position the belt loop section against its back in the position that best suits your personal preference. In most cases that will be dead center, but with longer knives you'll have enough latitude to position the belt loop so the knife rides high or low on your hip. Once you have the belt loop where you want it, hold it in place between thumb and forefinger and release the knife, laying the unfolded holster on a flat surface.

Now sew the belt loop to the back of the holster using a large needle and thread that matches the color of the strapping. Any type of sewing thread will work, but if you want maximum strength, use carpet thread or fly line. The stitch for this and the rest of the holster is a simple in-and-out "sine wave" stitch. For maximum strength, stitches should be no wider than one-eighth inch. Beginning as close to the edge of the belt loop as possible and about half an inch below the cut edge, run the row of stitches across its width at the top and bottom.The first stitch should be circled back upon itself at least twice to keep the thread ends from pulling through, or you can simply tie a knot in the end of the thread. When you've completed a row of stitches across the width of the strap, run a second row across from the opposite direction, on top of the first, to reinforce the seam.

With the belt loop attached, sew a two-inch strip of one-inch-wide Velcro to the front of what will be the knife pouch, about a half inch below the cut edge. A single row of short,

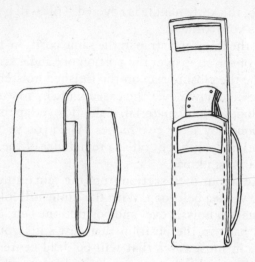

Many knife makers defeat the purpose of their own folding knives by offering them without belt holsters. The seat-belt holster shown here costs almost nothing to make and is more durable than most aftermarket holsters.

tight stitches around the strip's perimeter is usually sufficient to hold it in place, but I prefer to reinforce both mating strips with two additional rows of stitching forming an "X" across the strips' centers. Whether you fasten the hook or the loop half of the Velcro to the knife pouch doesn't make any difference, just so long as both mating strips are securely sewn in place.

The next step is to fold the pouch section back over the knife to determine exactly where you want it, then sew the front and back sides of the holster together using the same doubled sine wave stitch. To further strengthen the knife pouch near its mouth, run several looped stitches through and around the outside edges of the folded strap on both sides.

The last step in assembling the holster is to attach a mating strip of Velcro material to the inside of the closure flap. For a custom fit, slide your knife into the pouch and pull the flap closed over it. When you've determined the best location for the opposite half of the fastener, open the pouch and sew the mating strip in place.

To prevent the cut edges of the strap from fraying, saturate the exposed fibers with epoxy adhesive or carpenter's glue and let it dry. Either of these will keep the ends from fraying with a stiff yet flexible bond, but 24-hour epoxy is best because it's impervious to water. Superglue is a poor choice because it creates a stiff, brittle edge that will break apart with use, allowing the fibers below it to fray. Searing the cut edges with a match or lighter will also work with some types of strapping, but gives poor results with seat-belt material.

After you've given the glue time enough to set, you'll have a custom-made folding-knife holster that will serve you well for years to come. In fact, I've been making my own for more than 10 years and have yet to wear one out or ruin it; I go through knives more quickly than I do the holsters made for them. Considering the price, fit, and durability of a homemade folding-knife carrier, it seems a waste of money to buy an inferior aftermarket version.

SECTION 6

FIREARMS

Special note to the Firearms section:

The information contained in the **Firearms** section is intended only for people who have experience and knowledge in handling firearms. Some of these projects and techniques may not be appropriate for certain models of firearms. Never work on a loaded gun. When handling a gun, never assume it is unloaded—always check first, to make sure. Read all manufacturer's instructions before handling firearms, and always follow all instructions pertaining to use, care, and maintenance as set forth by the manufacturer.

Handle your gun in a safe, responsible manner; always exercise caution and skill when handling firearms. Make certain that you are informed as to the proper steps in care and use of firearms. Make certain that your firearm is in good operating condition; use proper ammunition; and be sure that no obstructions are in the chamber or bore. Twice as many firearms accidents occur in the home as in the outdoors, so always maintain extra caution and care.

Make sure you are competent and understand the principles of a job before attempting it, and be sure to wear safety goggles when appropriate. Do not attempt any project beyond your capabilities. If in doubt regarding any of the procedures in the **Firearms** section, stop immediately and consult a qualified gunsmith, or the manufacturer of the firearm.

SIGHTING-IN A RIFLESCOPE

Most of the hunters I know don't understand how to sight-in their own rifles, even though some have been hunting for years. Having your riflescope boresighted with a collimator is a poor substitute for actually zeroing your rifle on a range—although your local gunsmith will be happy to do it for about $5.00 a crack—and few "iron" sights can be trusted to hold their zero from one hunting trip to the next. Bouncing over rough roads in the trunk of a car can knock the best scopes or sights out of alignment, while just loading in fresh cartridges from a different lot than the one with which a gun was sighted can change your bullets' point of impact considerably. Any serious rifleman will tell you there are an awful lot of variables to consider in the quest for accuracy and while many are almost insignificant by themselves, all can work cumulatively against accuracy. Anyone who hunts with a gun has an obligation to make certain it can do the required job as effectively as possible.

Let's begin by assuming you've just bought a new scope for your rifle (we'll also assume that the base and rings are already in place). The first step is to mount the scope on the rings just snugly enough to allow the scope tube to slide between them. Pull the rifle to your shoulder as if you were about to shoot and slide the scope back and forth until the sight picture is as large and bright as you can get it. This is called "eye relief," and most scopes are designed to allow about four inches of it between the shooter's eye and the focal lens. You've achieved the proper eye relief when you can throw the rifle to your shoulder and instantly see a clear, well-lighted sight picture. If the picture looks fuzzy, loosen the locking ring located just forward of the eye bell and turn the eyepiece until the sight picture becomes sharp, then retighten the locking ring against the eye bell.

Don't tighten the rings down yet. Next you need to make certain the crosshairs are precisely perpendicular and horizontal to the rifle's sighting plane. This is critical because your eye will automatically tell your hands to adjust the horizontal crosshair parallel to the terrain you see through the scope. If

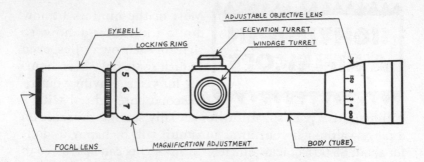

Anatomy of a typical variable-power telescopic sight.

your crosshairs are leaning slightly to the left, you'll tip, or "cant," the rifle to the right to compensate, which will in turn cause your shots to pull to the right. And if the crosshairs are leaning right, your shots will pull left.

Once you have the eye relief and crosshairs properly adjusted, snug down the ring screws and systematically check to be sure that all other mounting screws are tight. Bear in mind that most scope mounts and rings sold today are made from anodized aluminum alloy, not steel, and that too much torque can strip the threads. On the other hand, loose mounts guarantee a loss of accuracy that can be extreme sometimes. A rule of thumb I follow is "snug plus a quarter turn," which seems to work fine for everyone.

I should mention here that all scopes are designed to have the windage (left/right) adjustment turret on the right side when mounted to a rifle, which means that the elevation turret is on top. But top-eject guns like the Model 94 Winchester lever-action often require that the scope be rotated 90 degrees counterclockwise, which places the elevation turret to the left and the windage turret on top. This is done to allow ejected brass to clear the scope as it's being kicked from the breech. If the scope isn't oriented that way, empty casings will frequently hit the windage turret during ejection and fall right back into the breech, causing the action to jam. This problem is unique to top-eject rifles, and if yours is one, just remember that turning the windage adjustment, which now controls elevation, to the right will raise your bullet's point of impact, while turning the elevation adjustment up will move the bullet left. Aside from being mounted backward the turret adjustments function in exactly the same way—it's just that left becomes down and down becomes right.

Now that your scope is mounted, the next step is a trip to the range. You'll need a good target, like the Hoppe's S-5 sighting target, which is laid out in one-inch grids to take the guesswork out of sight adjustment. To help ensure consistency, you should also make sure that the cartridges you'll be using for sighting and hunting are all from the same lot (lot numbers are usually printed on the end flap of the box). A roll of masking tape for patching bullet holes will extend the useful life of your targets, and a felt-tip marker is handy for identifying groups or making notes on the targets.

To begin, I recommend firing a three-shot group into the first target from just 12 yards (or paces). Fire each round as carefully as you would from 100 yards, aiming not for the bullseye, but for the *center* of the bullseye. At this range, one inch of adjustment will require 32 clicks of the scope turret in the appropriate direction. For example, if the center of your group prints two inches to the right, adjust the windage turret left 64 clicks (32 clicks per inch × 2 inches = 64 clicks). The same goes for elevation, but because you're shooting from such a short distance, adjust the elevation to hit about four inches above the bullseye, with the windage dead center on the target. The point of this exercise is to get your shots "on paper" at 100 yards, and if you follow these instructions, they will be.

After you've made the required sight adjustments at 12 yards, move back to 100 yards and fire another three-shot group, again at the center of the bullseye and from a steady rest. *Never* shoot "offhand" from a standing position during the sighting process: you're not adjusting the shooter, only the sights. Turn a variable-power scope to its highest magnification to make the target appear larger, and to help you select an aiming point more precisely.

At 100 yards, scope adjustments are made at the rate of four clicks to each inch of travel. If 100 yards is your final sighting

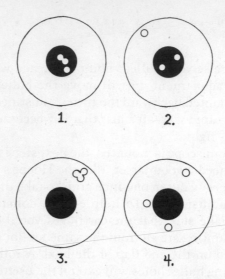

Analyzing your targets: (1) An ideal group has all shots in the center and grouped close together, indicating that rifle, shooter, and ammunition all function correctly. (2) A good two-shot group with a "flyer"—sometimes caused by erratically loaded ammunition, but more often by a shooter who simply jerked the trigger. (3) A very tight group of shots off-center on a target indicates that shooter and gun are doing their job, but the sights need adjustment. (4) A large, dispersed group of shots nearly always indicates that a shooter needs practice.

range, as it should be if your caliber is in the .30-.30 category, and the center of your group is three inches high, bring the elevation down 12 clicks. Likewise, if your group is five inches to the left, adjust the windage turret 20 clicks to the right. You may want to sight-in long-range calibers (.243, .270, and so on) for 200 yards; the rate of adjustment will be two clicks per inch.

The ultimate goal when shooting groups is to put every bullet through the same hole. That almost certainly won't happen, but every rifle or carbine on the market is capable of consistently shooting three-inch, three-shot groups at 100 yards, and most can do considerably better than that. If your groups are wider than three inches, your scope mounting screws are tight, and your rifle is in good condition, then the problem isn't your rifle. Like anything else, good marksmanship demands practice and discipline. If your shots print all over the target at 100 yards, don't blame your gun or its sights.

Knowing how to mount and sight-in your own scope will save costly trips to the gunsmith, as well as make you a far more effective hunter. Even the most expert marksman can't shoot well if his or her sights are off.

TELESCOPIC SIGHT DATA

Yards	Clicks Per Inch	One Click Equals
12.5	32	$\frac{1}{32}''$
25	16	$\frac{1}{16}''$
50	8	$\frac{1}{8}''$
75	6	$\frac{1}{6}''$
100	4	$\frac{1}{4}''$
200	2	$\frac{1}{2}''$
400	1	$1''$

Please note that these two procedures (glass bedding the action and floating the barrel) might recommend dismantling your gun further than what the manufacturer would recommend in the owner's manual as part of normal maintenance. Do so only at your own risk and with experience, skill, and caution—these are not projects for novices. Make sure you are competent and understand the principles of these jobs before attempting them. If in doubt, stop and consult a qualified gunsmith.

RIFLES THAT WON'T SHOOT STRAIGHT

Some rifles just won't shoot straight. It doesn't matter which brand of ammunition or weight of bullet is used, it doesn't matter whether the rifle is benchrested or fired off-hand, and it doesn't matter how skilled the shooter is. Some rifles simply refuse to consistently print well on a target—or on game.

In most cases these rifles are older, usually military, center-fire bolt-actions. Mausers, Enfields, and even the venerable Springfield '03-A3 in .30-06 caliber are all members of a group that exhibits varying degrees of accuracy. This may help to explain why one of two equally skilled shooters will snub a particular type of rifle while the other swears by it.

I encountered this problem firsthand several years ago when I was given a Mauser 98 chambered for the 7×57mm cartridge as a Christmas present. I had always wanted one of these fine, strong rifles, in spite of the fact that they're all right-handed and I'm not. The rifle had been sporterized using the original stock, which had been hand checkered and given a very classy looking Schnabel forend. The old military rear ramp sight had been replaced by a Williams micro-click adjustable sight. The rifle's only obvious shortcoming was that the original military trigger assembly had a monstrously heavy pull, with considerable creep before it released. Still, I could live with the trigger, at least until I could replace it with a match trigger assembly. I was anxious to see how this latest addition to my firearms collection performed on paper.

I had my chance a week later. It was a bright, sunny winter day with clear visibility and no wind. I set the first target at 100 yards and, using the hood of my truck as a benchrest with a sandbag supporting the rifle's forend, fired the first three-shot group using 175-grain spitzer-point bullets. The stock felt comfortable, the sights were clearly visible, and the trigger was manageable. When I traded the rifle for a pair of 10x50 binoculars after firing the first group, I felt confident that all three shots would be in the black.

Boy was I wrong. The group measured more than 10 inches across. Now I'm no Sergeant York, but I can shoot better than that on a stormy day with a sprained trigger finger and a migraine.

Subsequent groups were as bad as the first, or worse. During one I put two consecutive shots through the bullseye, only to have the third print off-target. Despite my best efforts, each group exhibited an unpredictability that would baffle even a Mensa statistician. I was fairly sputtering as I cased the Mauser and tossed it none too gently behind the seat of my truck.

Doubtless more than a few hunters and shooters can relate to this experience. Perhaps it's an heirloom .303 Enfield handed down by Grandpa, or maybe it's Dad's old .30-06 Springfield, but there must be hundreds, even thousands of old rifles gathering dust in closets because they just don't provide the consistent accuracy necessary to earn a shooter's trust. It's hard to understand how Dad or Grandpa put so much meat on the table with a rifle that shoots so erratically.

The truth is, these rifles were probably quite accurate when they were new, even with imprecise military sights and triggers. Chances are the problem doesn't have a thing to do with the sights, worn rifling, headspacing, or other problems often associated with inaccuracy. In almost every case I've seen the problem lies in the wood, not the metal.

A likely cause for inaccuracy in an older rifle is a loose fit between the action (not the barrel) and the stock. When these older rifles were manufactured, linseed oil was the wood preservative of choice. In fact, it was about the only choice. Shooters needed some type of wood preservative to prevent their gunstocks from drying out, warping, or rotting in a tropical environment. Linseed oil did that, and it had the added advantage of providing an attractive finish that brought out the natural beauty of the wood.

The down side, which wasn't immediately apparent, was that linseed oil also saturated and softened the wood. Repeated poundings from recoil eventually enlarged the inletted openings in the stock wherever the action contacted wood. This was particularly critical when it happened around the barrel lug inlet and screw. The end result is that the action actually moves during recoil, moving the barrel with it and changing the bullet's point of impact. And of course the variation grows progressively worse as the range increases.

The cure for a recoil-worn stock is to have the action "glass-bedded." This operation is performed by applying a thin layer (about one-eighth inch) of mixed epoxy resin to the wood surfaces where the action rests—*only* the action; don't apply resin to the barrel channel. When all the action recesses in the stock have been covered with resin, coat the action with a light film of "mold release" compound (petroleum jelly works fine) to keep it from adhering to the epoxy, and then reseat it into the stock. The barrel lug screw (also coated with petroleum jelly) is then tightened down snugly to ensure a proper fit. Any excess resin that squeezes out when the barrel lug screw is tightened can be wiped off with a cloth and a little solvent before it dries.

Screwing the action back into the stock displaces the uncured resin and forces it to form around the contours of the action. Leave the assembled rifle to dry for a *minimum* of 24 hours before removing the action from the stock and cleaning it. The action will require a bit of wiggling to free, but then that's the whole point of glass-bedding. With the action out, you'll see that the stock recesses are now form-fitted and mate exactly with every contour of the receiver. You can remove excess dried resin by carefully scraping it off with a razor knife. The resin should cure *at least 48 hours* before you fire the rifle.

When you reassemble the gun, be sure to include all original parts and pieces—make certain you have no integral parts leftover.

The second most common cause of inaccuracy in older rifles occurs in the barrel channel of the stock. When a centerfire rifle discharges, the barrel actually expands a few thousandths of an inch as hot gases force the bullet through it. If the stock presses against the barrel from any direction during this momentary expansion it will force the muzzle to change position, thereby changing the point of impact of the bullet. I encountered that problem a couple of years back with an old 1938 Russian Mosin-Nagant sniper rifle in 7.62×54 caliber. At 100 yards, the first shot drilled the bullseye, but subsequent rounds consistently printed progressively higher and farther to the right as the barrel expanded from heat.

Checking for this problem is as simple as inserting a 2×6-inch slip of paper lengthwise into the barrel channel between the stock and barrel. It should slide freely around the barrel to emerge on the opposite side. In this position the paper should slide unimpeded along the entire length of the barrel from the receiver to the end of the stock. If there isn't enough room at any point to fit the paper between the stock and barrel, I guarantee the muzzle is shifting position to some degree during discharge.

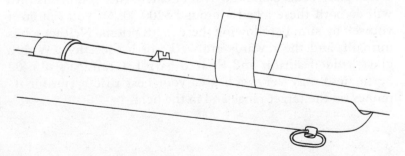

Check for proper clearance between the barrel channel and barrel by simply inserting a slip of paper between them. The paper should slide freely, without catching, from the receiver to the end of the stock.

The remedy for this affliction—which should be performed only after the action is bedded—is an operation known as "floating" the barrel. That simply means that the radius of the barrel channel is enlarged using wood chisels and a gunsmith's barrel channel rasp (I've even used a pocket knife and 50-grit sandpaper, but I don't recommend that approach) until the barrel has visible clearance all around the barrel channel. When satisfactory clearance has been achieved smooth the channel with sandpaper. When you've reassembled the gun, again, be sure that you've included everything—make certain you have no original, integral parts leftover.

Most gunsmiths actually use a bit of overkill when floating a barrel, opening the clearance to about ¹⁄₁₆ inch (approximately .062) all the way around. This is fine. The sole purpose of a stock's forend is to provide a comfortable handhold during firing. The stock should never make contact with the barrel, nor should you ever rest the barrel on anything while shooting, as this will almost certainly cause your bullets to deflect upward.

Modern bolt-action rifles, like the Model 70 Winchester, come from the factory with a glass-bedded stock and floated barrel. These are incredibly accurate right out of the box, easily and consistently plugging a bottle cap at 100 yards without modification.

But if you have an old military bolt-action too inaccurate to qualify as a serious hunting gun, it probably needs to have the action glass-bedded and the barrel floated. Any good gunsmith will do both these jobs for around $200.00. Or you can do it yourself by simply following these instructions. Neither job is difficult, and the rewards are well worth the effort. With a glass-bedded action and floated barrel, Grandpa's old '03 Springfield may very well give your best rifle a run for its money on the target range and in the field.

HOMEMADE BIKINI SCOPE COVERS

MATERIALS NEEDED:

▼

Latex rubber glove(s)

Most everyone who hunts these days uses a telescopic sight. In many cases optical sights have replaced iron sights altogether, which is understandable considering the many advantages they provide. Modern scopes are usually pretty rugged, but they do require a bit more care than iron sights, no part more so than the lenses. The difference between a very good scope and a mediocre scope is most often the lenses—or, more specifically, the delicate metallic coatings applied to them. These microscopically thin coatings are at least as important to a scope's clarity and light-gathering ability as the size of its tube or objective lens, and they need protection. For that reason, and because even the best lenses can become temporarily useless after a few minutes' exposure to driving rain or snow, every scope needs a sealed lens cover.

There are many types of factory-made scope covers on the market, from Butler Creek's superb flip-up models with spring-loaded covers that swing up at a touch of the thumbs to a simple pair of plastic cups attached by elastic bands. But even the best cover can be lost or damaged in the field, which is the place where your optics most need protection. Having a spare lens cover can be invaluable for keeping rain, snow, or—worst of all—pine sap from clouding your sight picture at that critical moment. Fortunately, rubber "bikini" scope covers (which retail for about $6.00) are easy to make at no cost and compact enough to carry in a jacket pocket.

The best medium I've found from which to make bikini lens covers is the wrist portion of latex rubber gloves, the kind used to protect hands from solvents and other chemicals. Most of us have a pair of these gloves lying around the basement, but re-

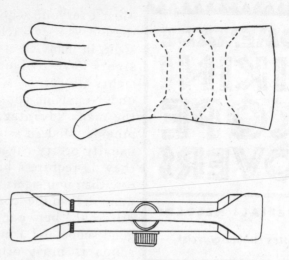

Bikini scope covers made from discarded rubber gloves are every bit as functional as their manufactured counterparts, but cost nothing to make.

member always to handle used gloves carefully until you've washed them thoroughly.

The rest is easy. Just lay the wrist portion of the glove on a flat surface and use sharp scissors to cut a three-inch-wide band crosswise from its width (see illustration). Stretched over the length of the scope, the resulting rubber band will protect your scope's lenses as well as any of the commercial bikini-type covers. The light, stretchy latex will completely cover and conform to the contours of either end to form a snug, watertight seal that stays put but can be quickly released for shooting. It should not be so tight that the molded rubber eye ring around the focusing lens is crushed or distorted. If that happens, try overstretching the band a few times by hand to relieve some of its tension.

Most any type or color of latex glove will work for making bikini scope covers, and the wrist portion of most gloves will yield two to three of them each, depending on the diameter of your scope's objective lens. Just make sure that the tube at either end of the scope is entirely covered with about a quarter inch of excess rubber all around; this ensures a good seal. As a bonus, the glove's fingers and thumb can be similarly cut to provide a number of wide, strong rubber bands that you'll no doubt find hundreds of uses for. Nor should you discard the cup-shaped finger and thumb tips; these can be stretched over the muzzle of a shotgun or heavy-barreled rifle to form excellent shoot-off muzzle caps. And all that utility from a "disposable" rubber glove.

FIELD-EXPEDIENT SHOOTING RESTS

Any serious rifleman will tell you that one of the best aids to accurate shooting is a steady rest. Olympic and other competitive shooters may be required to shoot from the offhand (standing) position, but when a shot must count in real life, even the best will find some means of steadying the rifle. All else being equal, the toughest variable to control in any sharpshooting system is always the shooter.

Installing a factory-made bipod is one way to provide a steady shooting platform in the field, but this has its drawbacks. Even the famed Harris Ultralight bipod adds a pound of weight to a rifle, and I've yet to see a bipod that wasn't more trouble than it was worth in the field. Worse yet are "barrel bipods" designed to attach directly to the rifle's barrel. Resting your rifle's weight by its barrel on a bipod or anything else is guaranteed to make it shoot high and defeats the purpose of having a bipod in the first place.

Probably the most workable solution is the field-expedient tripod used by military snipers—in fact, at least one Marine

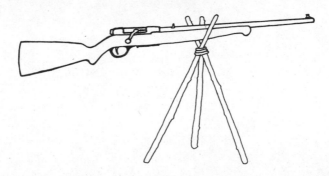

Field-expedient tripods and other shooting rests provide as much accuracy as commercial rests. In fact, one military sniping instructor reportedly refuses to let his students use anything else.

Corps sniper instructor is said to allow his students to use nothing else. This very simple shooting rest consists of nothing more than three sticks, each about one inch in diameter and two to three feet long, held together by a loose wrap of cord or rope. Once it's assembled, spreading the legs of the tripod to form a triangle will also spread the top of the tripod to form a convenient crotch in which to rest the rifle. Being bound together gives the three legs a scissorslike action; the shooting rest will become very stable under the rifle's weight. The height of the shooting platform is easily adjusted up or down by sliding the wrapped cord along the length of the three legs.

An equally easy-to-make but slightly less stable shooting platform is the "sniper stick," a simple Y-shaped branch shoved into the ground, crotch-up. Laying the stock of your rifle in this crotch provides an acceptably steady rest, and the sniper stick can be adjusted for height by varying how much of the lower leg you shove into the ground. For obvious reasons this type of shooting rest cannot be used in snow or when the ground is frozen.

A third type of field-expedient shooting rest is the "Moses stick," so called because it vaguely resembles the staff the Biblical hero wielded so effectively against his enemies. In this instance, however, the only trick performed by the Moses stick is furnishing a standing shooter with a positive rifle rest. Basically a six-foot walking stick with several inches of a horizontal branch left attached to form a crotch, the Moses stick is well suited for opportunistic hunters, especially those caught in a survival situation where hiking and hunting go hand-in-hand. Properly fitted, the Moses stick allows its owner to make fast, accurate shots in tall grass without having to fire offhand or search frantically for a suitable tree branch.

Of course, in a pinch using any type of shooting rest is better than shooting offhand, be it a tree branch, stump, or one of the conventional sitting, kneeling, or prone positions. But with a little practice, field-expedient shooting rests, particularly the tripod, can deliver near-benchrest accuracy using nothing more than the tools provided by nature.

RANGER SLING

MATERIALS NEEDED:

▼

50'–100' 550-lb. nylon parachute cord

▼

Rifle or shotgun with sling swivels

Anyone who lugs a rifle or shotgun around the woods in pursuit of game appreciates the convenience of a carry sling on his or her firearm. Not only does a sling permit you to carry the gun over a shoulder or across the back, leaving your hands free, but accomplished riflemen will tell you that "getting into the sling" by wrapping it around the forearm of your support hand will help to keep the muzzle steady when making long-range offhand shots. And I like seeing slings on hunting firearms because their swivel positions virtually guarantee that the muzzle will be pointed in a safe direction with the gun at the carry.

But what if you could have a rifle sling that not only functioned as an ordinary gun carrier, but could also be used to splint an injured limb, fashion an emergency tourniquet, replace a broken bootlace, make a pair of emergency snowshoes, drag out a downed whitetail, and even hang the deer for skinning? It's called a "Ranger sling" after the elite military group that conceived of it. Trained to be self-sufficient in any environment, the Rangers demand lightweight, straightforward field gear with as much utility built into every component as possible. The Ranger sling certainly fits that description.

But don't rush off to the nearest sporting goods store just yet, because while the Ranger sling might be the epitome of multifunctionality in wilderness equipment, not a single manufacturer produces it. The good news is that to make one you need only patience, about an hour of your time, and 50 to 100 feet of 550-pound test nylon parachute cord. Both military-spec and lighter strength civilian parachute cord are available from most outfitters, army-navy stores, and outdoors mail-order companies. But if paracord is unavailable, the Ranger sling can be made from duck decoy cord or even clothes line.

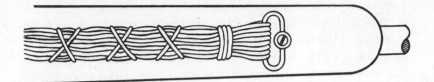

A close-up of the Ranger sling, showing its construction.

Probably the easiest method of making the Ranger sling is to put it directly onto the gun that will carry it, without removing the sling swivels. Start by laying out the cord you'll be using, tying one end to the buttstock swivel with a double half-hitch knot. Run the opposite end of the cord through the forearm swivel, then back through the buttstock swivel, and pull the remainder of the cord after it. You now have a complete loop connecting both swivels. The finished Ranger sling is not adjustable (but then, when was the last time you needed to adjust the sling on your deer gun?), so the first two or three loops made between the swivels are pulled to the desired carry length and used as a gauge for subsequent loops.

After the initial loops have been adjusted for length, the process becomes a simple, if somewhat tedious matter of running the free end of the cord back and forth through the two swivels. At this point, I prefer to hook the developing sling over a doorknob, where the (unloaded!) firearm's own weight will help to maintain constant length and tension on the cord as successive loops are added.

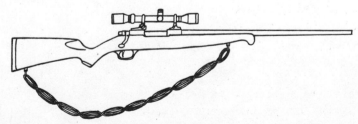

The Ranger sling, made from parachute cord or rope, is simple, quiet in the bush, and more versatile than any gun sling on the market.

When you've run all but about eight feet of cord through the swivels, the final step is to bind the loose sling together by wrapping the remaining cord around it in a spiral fashion from one end to the other. When the spirals reach the opposite end, loop the cord through the swivel and wrap a series of spirals in the other direction, tying off the loose end at the swivel. You now have a fully functional Ranger sling. To improve its esthetics, leave enough extra cord to fashion a tightly wrapped carrying handle in the center of the sling. And don't be afraid to experiment; there are any number of ways to complete the final step. With a little ingenuity you can create a handsome finished product that looks as good on a Weatherby as it does on a bare-bones survival .22.

Aside from the obvious fact that the Ranger sling provides a ready supply of stout cord, it also works exceptionally well for carrying a firearm. The bundled cord feels soft and cushiony against the shoulder and won't dig in or chafe the way strap-type slings can. Even better for hunters, there are no buckles, hooks, or rivets to make noise during those moments when absolute silence is critical. Best of all, for admitted cheapskates like myself the cost of this truly multifunctional hunting accessory is about $4.00, or about half the price of a basic, no-frills manufactured rifle sling that won't do anything except carry your gun.

Make sure you are competent and understand the principles of this job before attempting it. Do not attempt any project beyond your capabilities. Never work on a loaded gun, and never assume a gun is unloaded—check it first, to make sure. If in doubt regarding any procedures here, stop and consult a qualified gunsmith.

CLEANING ROD BORE GUIDE

MATERIALS NEEDED:
▼
Wooden dowel

Experienced riflemen know that one of the imperatives of good marksmanship is frequent and thorough cleaning, which keeps the rifling grooves in their barrels polished and sharp; in fact, the USMC sniper school recommends that trainees clean their rifles every five rounds. But they also realize that they need to exercise the utmost care to keep the cleaning rod and its attachments from gouging the bore. A scratch in the bore, or, more seriously, a nick in the muzzle crown, will adversely affect accuracy by causing the expanding gases to exert uneven pressure against the bullet as they drive it through the barrel. The end result is bullet "yaw," a deviation from horizontal axis during flight that means the projectile flies obliquely instead of straight at the target. The chamber wall likewise must be protected during cleaning, because scratches in it will eventually lead to extraction problems.

As protection against bore damage, sharpshooters have long realized that every rifle, design permitting, should be cleaned from the breech end, never the muzzle end. Even though modern aluminum cleaning rods are softer than their steel predecessors, to minimize bore damage, professional riflemen hedge their bets by using a plug-type guide to keep the cleaning rod from wobbling as it passes through the barrel. The guide, which replaces a rifle's bolt in the breech, virtually guarantees that nothing but brush bristles or a patch will contact the bore walls.

Manufactured bore guides are available from a few companies, most notably MTM Case-Gard, but these cost about $6.00 apiece, and you can make one that works just as well for far less money. The most common medium from which to make a bore guide is a simple wooden dowel, available in four-foot lengths from most any lumber supply outlet for about $3.00, depending on diameter. Just one dowel will yield 8 to 12 bore guides, so you'll never have to worry about having one on hand when cleaning your tack-driver. The diameter of the dowel you choose will of course depend on the diameter of your gun's bolt, but for the sake of simplicity, half-inch dowel will work as is in most .22s, while the majority of .30 calibers will accept three-quarter-inch. For a more precise fit, I've found it's best to start with a slightly oversized dowel and sand it down until it exactly matches the inside diameter of the breech. Ideally, the bore guide should match your rifle's bolt diameter and length as closely as possible.

The length of dowel you cut off to make the bore guide depends on the type of rifle you have. For example, some .22 rifles have an integral ejector rod/bolt guide that won't allow a dowel to be inserted from the rear of the receiver with the bolt removed. In this case, the bore guide must be inserted through the ejector port, the length of which will of course determine the length of the dowel section. That won't be a problem with most centerfire bolt-actions, whose receivers are usually obstruction-free once the bolt is removed. In any event, the bore guide should be as long as the action will permit, to give the cleaning rod as much support as possible as you stroke it back and forth through the barrel.

Once you've determined the length of bore guide your rifle will accept, cut off that section of dowel as squarely as possible and drill a hole through its exact center, from one end to the other (this is more easily and accurately done using a drill press). Once again, the diameter of the hole drilled through the dowel depends on the diameter of your cleaning rod, which

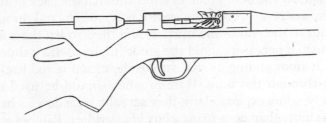

Scratching the chamber, bore, or muzzle crown of any rifle with a cleaning rod will degrade its accuracy. Bore guides made from a simple wooden dowel will prevent such damage.

needs to slide through the bore guide freely but with as little clearance as possible. Cleaning rods for .22 and .30 calibers measure about .203 and .245 inch, respectively. Based on those dimensions, .22-caliber bore guides should have a hole diameter of $7/32$ inch (.219), while those intended for larger centerfire cleaning rods should be drilled at $17/64$ inch (.266). If the hole seems too small to accommodate your cleaning rod, don't redrill it to the next larger size until you've applied a liberal amount of gun oil to its inside wall. Oil will soften the wood slightly and lubricate the cleaning rod as it passes through. Remember, the idea is to hold the rod firmly, so a little snug is better than a little loose.

The final step in making a bore guide is to chamfer (bevel) the end that will be inserted into the gun's chamber at an angle steep enough to allow at least a quarter inch of the guide to fit inside the chamber mouth. This operation can be performed by hand with a disk or belt sander (or even just a piece of 50-grit sandpaper), but exercise care to keep the chamfer angle as even and concentric with the drilled hole as possible. The bore guide's resulting truncated shape will tend to center itself inside the chamber, and helps keep the delicate chamber mouth and walls from being nicked, which often leads to further extraction problems.

To use the bore guide, simply slide the rod through the hole in its center, attach a brush or patch jag to its end, and insert the assembly into the rear of your rifle's receiver. If your rifle won't allow the bore guide to enter through the back of the receiver, insert it through the ejector port, run the rod through it and out to the end of the muzzle, and then attach the bore jag or brush. If necessary, hold the guide in place with a thumb to keep it from sliding as you stroke the cleaning rod back and forth through the bore. Wire brushes should be used infrequently; some experts claim they actually wear down a barrel's rifling more than does firing a box of cartridges. Patches should be passed through the barrel only once and then discarded. Cleaning should continue until a patch emerges from the muzzle unsoiled.

Used religiously, the dowel-type bore guide will extend barrel life and maximize accuracy while protecting the bore and chamber walls from the damage that results from using an unguided cleaning rod. If your rifle has been glass-bedded, the bore guide will also act as a chamber plug to prevent cleaning solvents from dripping onto and damaging the epoxy bedding material. Making this valuable accessory is inexpensive and simple; once you've made one, you'll find you can create another in just minutes. It's a small price to pay for the security of knowing that the first (and in most cases only) round you fire at that trophy white-tailed deer will be as accurate as it can be.

Please note that this procedure might recommend dismantling your gun further than what the manufacturer would recommend in the owner's manual as part of normal maintenance. Do so only at your own risk and with experience, skill, and caution—this is not a project for novices. Make sure you are competent and understand the principles of this job before attempting it. If in doubt, stop and consult a qualified gunsmith.

WEATHERPROOF FIREARM FINISH

MATERIALS NEEDED:

▼
1 can black primer spray paint

▼
1 can clear, flat polyurethane spray

▼
1 can olive drab or hunter green spray paint (optional)

▼
1 can brown spray paint (optional)

When a good friend and I took off for a weekend of camping and squirrel hunting a few years back, the weatherman had predicted sunny skies for the duration. He lied. No sooner had we reached our campsite Friday evening than the sky turned black and low, and angry thunder began rolling our way. We barely had time to get a shelter erected over ourselves and our backpacks before the skies opened and sheets of hard, steady rain began pummeling anything not under a roof.

It was still pouring the next morning as we sat in gloomy silence spooning up a breakfast of canned fruit cocktail. Suddenly Bill shot me a look of slack-jawed horror, as though he'd just remembered that today was his wedding anniversary, and ran out into the rain. He returned a few seconds later with his brand-new 12-gauge pump shotgun, its handsome bluing now streaked with ugly brown rust. The poor man was almost in tears as he tried to rub the gun's metalwork back to its previous luster with his jacket sleeve. He succeeded only in getting his sleeve dirty, but I took advantage of the distraction by eating the rest of his fruit cocktail.

Finally it dawned on him that I wasn't the least concerned about my own gun. "Hey," he said, pointing to where my battered but completely unrusty .22 hung barrel-down with water dripping from its front sight, "how come *your* gun isn't rusty?"

The answer was, mine was a survival rifle, equipped and expected to perform reliably under the worst conditions of weather and neglect for extended periods. Its "bluing" was actually a hard black matte finish composed of several layers of flat black primer and clear polyurethane—impervious to water, scratch-resistant, and nonreflective. I've been applying this finish (with a few improvements along the way) to every long gun I've owned for more than a decade and have become so accustomed to simply ignoring the external surface of my guns that I wouldn't have it any other way.

Begin by removing the gun's action from the stock. Next, prepare the barreled action for priming by stripping all traces of oil from its outer surfaces. You can use a "hot" solvent, like automotive brake or carburetor cleaner, but I prefer dishwashing soap, a synthetic scouring pad, and very hot water. Using soap and water takes a little longer, but it's just as effective and a lot more considerate of the environment. When the oil is gone the gun metal will take on a dull, almost gray appearance.

Before applying the first coat of primer, consider which parts of the assembly you don't want coated. Little is gained by priming the bolt or the inside of the receiver, because these will be scraped bare after the action has cycled a few times, leaving a gummy residue that does nothing for the gun's performance. And you should definitely avoid getting paint inside the chamber, as this can cause jamming, especially with autoloaders. In most cases, removing the bolt and inserting a rolled piece of paper in its place will adequately protect the firearm's inner workings. It's also a good idea to plug the rifle's muzzle with a cleaning patch to keep from fouling that particularly critical section of rifling. Other parts you'd like to keep unpainted, such as the trigger and sights, can be covered carefully with tape. A rifle with a scope can be coated as a single unit by covering each end of the scope with a square of sticky duct tape to protect the delicate lenses, and by making sure the turret caps are snug.

At this point I like to suspend the stripped receiver from a cord tied through the trigger guard or, barring that, around the barrel lug. This ensures equal access to all external surfaces and helps the primer to dry evenly. Primer should be sprayed on in thin coats, with each layer being allowed to dry completely before the next is applied (about thirty minutes between coats). I recommend applying at least three coats of primer to guarantee adequate coverage and protection.

When the primer coat has dried thoroughly, spray on two to three coats of clear, flat polyurethane, giving each coat at least three hours to dry before applying the next. The resulting finish will have a slightly rough, pebble-grain look and feel that's not only attractive, but easy to hang onto in the rain and nonreflective in bright sunlight.

If you'd prefer to camouflage the receiver and barrel assembly, just spray diagonal stripes of green and brown paint across the primer with quick, smooth strokes. Ideally, this should be done before the polyurethane finish coats are put on.

Next comes the stock. First remove the buttplate, floorplate, swivels, and any other metalwork, and give each piece the same treatment you gave the barrel and receiver. If your rifle has a separate trigger assembly, take care not to get primer or polyurethane on its inner workings, as this almost certainly will add a couple of pounds to the trigger pull for the first several rounds.

With the stock's metalwork removed, all of its inletted crevices and channels will be exposed. You may find that the factory missed a few areas when the stock was treated. If you'd like to leave the stock with a smooth wood-grain finish, just give it two or three light coats of clear or glossy polyurethane (your choice), taking care that any untreated internal surfaces are well sealed. Once again, I recommend suspending the stock by a cord or on a long peg to provide better access to all its surfaces without having to touch it.

If you'd prefer a camouflage finish on the stock, first remove, or at least rough up, the original finish with sandpaper, then give it three light coats of black primer. When the primer coats are dry, you can then add diagonal brown and green stripes for a dark, subdued pattern that blends very well with most types of wooded terrain. Or you might choose to cover the primer with a base coat of hunter or olive green before adding contrasting stripes of brown and black. Feel free to experiment with patterns. If you find you can't live with your artwork, you can always apply another base coat and start over on a clean slate.

Note that wood stocks treated with linseed or other oils are a poor choice for camouflaging: their pores are saturated with a medium to which nothing, including epoxy, will adhere. Oil finishes are generally found on those older guns made before modern polymers were invented, especially military rifles like the M98 Mauser, .303 British, or Springfield '03-A3. The finish described here will adhere to them as well as anything can, but oil-saturated wood will eventually cause it to peel away.

After you've camouflaged the stock to your satisfaction, give it time to dry completely before applying three to four final coats of polyurethane inside and out. This will encapsulate the entire stock inside tough plastic and give it the same mildly rough finish the barrel and receiver have. I suggest allowing all the components to dry for a minimum of 24 hours before reassembling them. When you do reassemble the firearm, be sure you have no original parts leftover when you're done. The result will be a handsome firearm whose external surfaces will refuse to rust, crack, or warp under any conditions and will scratch or chip only with excessive abuse.

Most sporting guns will never see the treatment needed to damage this finish. But working guns like the old rat-shooters farmers keep in their barns or the jeep guns carried by ranchers may receive enough hard knocks to expose small portions of metal or wood. These battle scars are easily touched up with a shot of spray enamel followed by a spot coat of polyurethane.

Best of all, this protection is downright cheap. An initial outlay of about $15.00 for materials will weatherproof a dozen guns, which works out to just $1.25 per application. Compare that to the price of Teflon and other commercial coatings that can cost in the hundreds of dollars for a single gun. This weatherproof firearm finish would be a deal even if it didn't work as well as any of them.

SECTION 7

SURVIVAL

SOAP-DISH SURVIVAL KIT

MATERIALS NEEDED:

▼

Plastic soap dish

▼

*Butane lighter
and/or matches*

▼

Firestarter

▼

Pocket compass

▼

*Topographical map,
weatherproofed*

▼

Folding knife

▼

Cord

▼

Fishing line and tackle

▼

Tweezers

▼

*Your choices of other survival
equipment*

I'd bet not one person who ever became lost or stranded in the forest expected it to happen. No snowmobiler believes he or she might throw a track or blow a piston 10 miles from the nearest plowed road. It always comes as a surprise to look around and realize that nothing is familiar, or that nightfall is a lot closer than the car. And you can believe that it's a real shock to suddenly be caught in a howling maelstrom of whipping, stinging snow with subzero winds that can make foot travel perilous, if not impossible. Yet situations like these pop up all the time and too few outdoorsmen are adequately prepared to take them in stride. Without a few basic necessities, molehills become mountains and what should be an inconvenience becomes life-threatening.

Survival kits are nothing new, nor does having one mean that its owner is a greenhorn woodsman. No one in their right mind would ever call Jim Bridger, Davy Crockett, John Colter, or Daniel Boone greenhorns, yet all carried a "possibles bag" over one shoulder whenever they ventured away from camp or cabin. The possibles bag contained the shot, powder, and wads needed to keep the frontiersman shooting, but it was also a handy place to carry flint, tinder, compass, and a few provisions.

The invention of unitized cartridge ammunition made the possibles bag obsolete and it was quickly abandoned, along with the survival tools it carried. Yet a working survival kit is as necessary as it ever was, except now its essential components are vastly superior to anything used by our ancestors. Compasses are more compact, lighter, and far more durable than ever before. We have at our disposal an array of accurate topographical maps to make navigation with the compass a snap. Flint and steel now take the form of manufactured tools like Gerber's superb Strike Force fire-starting kit. Today, all of us have the ability to be the best-equipped, most self-sufficient woodsmen in history, but only if we choose to exercise that option by preparing beforehand.

The trick is to make the personal survival kit easy to carry so there can be no excuse for leaving it behind. It has to be a self-contained unit small enough to fit easily in a breast pocket, yet functional enough to provide for as many of its owner's needs as possible. Small size and portability are important features for a personal survival kit because fate sometimes has a macabre sense of humor and the first time the kit is left behind will likely be the time it's really needed.

The personal survival kit I use and recommend to friends whose activities might take them beyond easy reach of civilization consists basically of a plastic soap dish packed with an assortment of small survival essentials. Plastic soap dishes are available in most drug or department stores for $1.00 each and both the one-piece type with hinged lid and the two-piece model with cover work well for putting together a personal survival kit. I personally prefer the two-piece type because it slides more easily into the GI compass pouch, which not only keeps the kit and its contents secure, but allows the kit to be ALICE-clipped to its owner's belt.

Of course, the utility of this or any survival kit is determined by the items inside. The ability to start a fire under any conditions is vitally important to the outdoorsman who may be forced to spend a night or two in the wilderness, particularly in cold weather. Matches are an option, but I prefer the butane lighter because there are 20 paper matches in a book and a thousand campfires in a Bic. The butane lighter also offers the advantage of being impervious to water, although the striker wheel and flint must be dry to make a spark. Paraffin-coated "Lifeboat" matches are also an option, but at an average price of $2.00 for 80 matches (usually two boxes of 40 each), they hardly compete with the $.79 butane lighter.

Under wet, windy, or very cold conditions the butane lighter or matches may prove insufficient to get a fire going and should be complemented by a modern, chemical fire-starting product. Military surplus Trioxane or Hexamine tablets and Gerber's Strike Force fuel bars are probably the best of these. All three burn with intense heat, produce no smoke, and have an almost invisible flame, and all are capable of starting a fire in the pouring rain (see "Starting A Fire, Regardless," page 12).

Next to go into the soap-dish survival kit is a quality liquid-filled pocket compass. You are never lost if you have a working compass and know even vaguely the direction of a road, railroad grade, or similarly large landmark. The compass need not be sophisticated or expensive, but it should be small and as well made as possible. Many modern compasses fit these criteria for under $20.00. Two very good choices are the American-made Brunton Tag-A-Long Plus, with integral thermometer and wind-chill chart, and the tiny folding Silva Huntsman with rotating bezel, map scale, and sundial. Both are rugged, high-quality navigation tools that will get you out of the woods, but bear in mind that we're talking about compact compasses for the survival kit, not full-sized orienteering instruments. Backpackers and hikers should always have a more versatile map compass like Brunton's highly functional model 8040 as their main instrument.

Whenever possible, the compass should be paired with a detailed map of the area you'll be traveling. A topographical map, usually available from local outfitters, is best because it shows terrain elevations, which can be very useful in helping the tired or injured hiker avoid swamps and tall hills. The map should also show the location of secondary roads, two-tracks, and marked trails. If for some reason a detailed map is unavailable, even the state maps sold by gas stations will suffice because any map is better than none at all.

The survival map differs from ordinary maps in that it must be weatherproof and completely impervious to water. Some of the new snowmobile trail maps are printed on a plastic-coated paper that holds up well under wet conditions and common paper maps can be sealed against the elements by laminating them with clear plastic contact paper, available in roll form from most department stores (see "Weatherproof Maps," page 64). Laminated maps are a bit more bulky, but very durable and absolutely waterproof, and they will not tear in even gale-force winds. They can also be marked with a crayon or grease pencil and then wiped clean for the next time they're needed.

The final yet by no means least important item in the soap-dish survival kit is a good, sharp folding knife. I prefer a three-blade stockman's knife like the Schrade Old Timer because its clip-point, sheepfoot, and penknife blades provide maximum utility in a compact package. The stockman's knife isn't a true survival knife, but it will skin, whittle, and cut well enough to perform many necessary chores in the wilderness, and it's easier to handle while skinning small game or cleaning fish than a larger belt knife. You can't pry, saw, chop, or hammer with it, but it has a place in the survival kit.

Even with these four most necessary components packed inside, there will still be sufficient room in the soap dish to add cord, fishing line and tackle, tweezers, and other small items. The general-purpose soap-dish survival kit that occupies a permanent place in the breast pocket of my field jacket contains the four items just mentioned, and there are five additional, more specific soap-dish kits in the small daypack I wear while hunting, snowshoeing, or just plain wandering through the swamps. The blue one is packed with emergency first-aid supplies; the red one is filled with needles, thread, cord, and a small pair of scissors; the white one is a miniature tacklebox, complete with jigging lures, flies, 100 feet of 20-pound test monofilament line, and a spare jackknife; the clear one contains a folding toothbrush, toothpaste, dental floss (this also works very well for emergency snares), and a small tube of Ora-Jel analgesic cream; the green soap dish carries extra Trioxane tablets, matches, a small butane lighter, fire wicks, and a three-

inch section of candle. Each of these kits is held securely shut
with a heavy rubber band and those in the daypack are further
sealed inside Ziploc bags.

But the survival kit in my coat pocket is without question
the most important of them all. That's the one that I know will
get me back to civilization through all but the worst weather
and luck. And if conditions demand that I spend a night or two
in the wilderness, this kit makes it possible for me to stay
warm, light a signal fire, or send a plume of smoke above the
trees as a signal to anyone who might be watching. I know that
it will always be there because I only take it out in emergencies
or when the coat is being washed (a couple of times the kit was
laundered as well, with no damage to its contents). The soap-
dish survival kit has become such a permanent fixture that I
barely notice it most of the time. But it's always there, always
at hand should I be forced to go to ground in foul weather or
suddenly find myself in unfamiliar terrain. It may not be large,
complex, or even expensive, but so long as I have it with me I
know I'll never be more than temporarily delayed in the woods.

SURVIVAL HARNESS

In my own experience, the factor that contributes most to the injuries and deaths that occur every year in the wilderness is a lack of proper equipment. Compared to even our most lowly animal brethren, *Homo sapiens* is a babe in the woods, a slow, clumsy biped with almost none of the physical or sensory attributes necessary for survival in a natural environment. Our sole advantage lies in the uniquely human ability to think abstractly and adapt quickly. While animals react to changes in their environment, we can anticipate them, and only we possess the mastery of tools that has allowed us to reach the top of the food chain.

Thanks to sometimes astounding leaps in technology, today's woodsman has at his disposal equipment that more than compensates for any lack of natural ability. But none of it can do any good unless you have it on your person at all times in the woods. For that reason, any really functional all-purpose survival kit must wear comfortably enough to become habit-forming, yet at the same time carry as much of the equipment required to address an infinite number of conditions as possible. For that job I haven't found anything that serves as well as the US Army's LBE (Load Bearing Equipment) harness.

At first glance there's nothing remarkable about the LBE harness. It consists only of a grommeted nylon pistol belt attached to a pair of heavy canvas or nylon suspenders. By itself it has little value as a survival tool, but it does provide an ideal place to attach the many individual kits that provide such versatility and value to a woodsman. My own harness boasts 10 such kits, each dedicated to a specific function, plus a survival knife, a Mini-Mag flashlight, two .45 ACP magazine pouches containing four .22 rifle clips, and a canteen with cup. Fully loaded it weighs just 10 easily carried pounds and if there's a situation beyond its capabilities, I haven't found it.

For carrying larger items that experience has shown to be worth toting into the woods—like needle-nosed pliers, a spool

of 20-pound fishing line, and Gerber's Strike Force firestarter—
I opt for two .30-caliber (M-14) magazine pouches. If you prefer,
smaller M-16 mag pouches will also work. The mag pouches
are positioned on the belt so that one rides over each hip, making them easily accessible while still providing the freedom to
shoot from a prone position or to belly crawl with a camera.
These and the other pouches on my harness are secured to the
belt with ALICE clips (an acronym for All-purpose Lightweight
Individual Carrying Equipment). The ALICE clips make adding
or detaching individual kits a quick and simple operation while
still keeping them securely in place through the roughest terrain.

The remaining eight kits are made from nylon GI compass
pouches with snap down flaps. One of them does indeed sport
a Brunton 8040 prismatic compass and a plastic-laminated
map, but the rest have been committed to other functions. Several years ago I discovered that a plastic two-piece soap dish fits
into the GI compass pouch almost as if the two were made for
each other. That made it possible to pack individual kits containing smaller items that might otherwise fall out through the
flap during the rigors of wilderness travel. An added advantage
is that these soap dishes are made in a variety of colors to make
identification of their contents possible at a glance. On my own
harness, for example, the red soap dish contains fire-starting
tinder and tools, the white one is filled with first-aid supplies,
the green one is packed with fishing gear, and the blue one
holds a personal AM-FM receiver.

To the right front shoulder strap of the suspenders (because
I'm left-handed), I've taped a USAF survival knife in the handle-
down position. This setup allows me to draw and resheath the
knife smoothly and quickly even in complete darkness. My
main knife, a Buck M-9 field knife, I carry on my trousers belt,
leaving the harness knife free for digging roots and other hard
jobs that might damage the edge of a knife I need to keep sharp.
To keep the survival knife from sliding downward along the suspender strap, I've tied the bottom of the sheath to the cross-strap
located at the front shoulder of each suspender. If necessary to
keep the knife from sliding out of its sheath, wrap the retaining

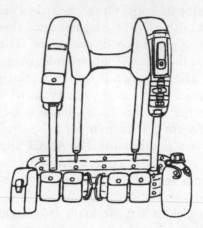

By itself, the US Army LBE harness has little value, but when loaded with pouches and other equipment it becomes the most valuable piece of survival gear this woodsman has ever owned.

strap that goes around the handle with safety tape or friction tape to reduce its inside diameter and make it fit more tightly.

The cost of my survival harness, minus the equipment it contains, was about $60.00. Suspenders retail for around $15.00, ammo pouches for $7.00 each, and compass pouches for about $2.00 apiece. Pistol belts sell for $10.00 to $14.00, depending on the type of buckle they use, while soap dishes can be found at most drug and department stores for less than a dollar. The USAF survival knife retails for approximately $20.00. If money is a bit tight, you don't have to start with a full-blown harness like mine to have a functional survival kit. I've been adding to and modifying my harness for more than 10 years, and since yours will reflect your own needs I've offered mine only as an example of how well a harness can be equipped.

Over the years I've put together and used a lot of different types of survival kits, from shoulder bags to fanny packs, and none has ever served as well as my fully equipped LBE harness. When I'm in the woods it's my constant companion whenever I'm not sleeping. It carries so easily I can almost forget it's there, yet experience has taught me that it's the most valuable piece of survival gear I own.

CATTAIL ROPE

When I wrote the book *Practical Outdoor Survival*, I recommended that survivalists forego making rope from plant fibers in favor of packing a bundle of stout nylon parachute cord into their survival kits. I still feel that way because ounce-for-ounce nothing you can make from available materials in nature compares to manufactured cord in terms of strength, durability, or pure utility. But because parachute cord is such a valuable commodity to anyone caught in a genuine survival situation, there might be times when it's expedient to conserve it by making use of natural rope materials. Rope made from natural vegetation is adequate for lashing together shelters, applying splints or tourniquets to injured limbs, and any number of other light-duty jobs that call for rope or cord.

Fibrous plant materials that lend themselves to rope making include the stringy inner bark of poplar and cedar trees, most grasses, and practically any plant whose stem separates into tough fibers when crushed. I've elected to use cattail leaves as an example because I believe they make a superior rope, are easily worked, and are readily available in virtually every part of the world that has water. Four-strand (approximately half-inch-diameter) cattail rope can support loads up to 100 pounds, ties fairly easily, and can be made in any length you might need. Bear in mind that only green cattail leaves will work for this project because dry leaves become brittle and tear too easily.

The secret to getting maximum strength out of any material used for rope making lies in the number of strands incorporated into the final product. Many small strands are stronger than a few large strands, so we'll begin by using single cattail leaves cut off near their bases and split lengthwise down their middles. The first step is to crush and separate the leaf's fibers by rolling it forcefully back and forth between your palms. Next, tie the two narrow ends of the split leaf together using three half-hitches for each half (see illustration). Leave the knots loose—their only function is to hold the two sections of

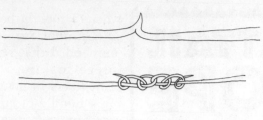

Top to bottom: (1) split the cattail leaf lengthwise; (2) tie the narrow ends of each half together using two half-hitches; (3) twist the tied leaf until it tends to wind around itself.

cattail leaf together during the next step in the process.

Stand on one end of the connected halves and pull the opposite end gently upward, just enough to take the slack out of it. For most of us, that means holding the upper end overhead, because the cattail leaf will now be approximately seven feet long. With your foot holding the bottom end securely against the ground, begin twisting the upper end in a clockwise direction. (It doesn't actually matter in which direction you twist the leaf, but it is important that each section be twisted in the same direction every time.) As you twist, the leaf will become shorter and more uniform along its length, but don't twist too tightly or the two halves will break apart. This is the most delicate stage of the rope-making process and you've applied enough tension when the leaf shows a tendency to coil around itself.

Next, maintaining tension from both ends, use the index finger of one hand to bend the twisted leaf in half at its middle, bringing the two ends together. You'll note that the two halves have a strong tendency to coil around themselves in the counterclockwise direction. Let them do just that, but allow it to happen slowly and smoothly, keeping both free ends together and the folded length taut. The result will be about three feet of two-strand twisted material that has begun to resemble rope. Repeat this process until you have several such lengths, or about twice the total length you think you'll need.

Now, you can't do a whole lot with three-foot lengths of double-strand rope, so the next step is to splice these lengths to-

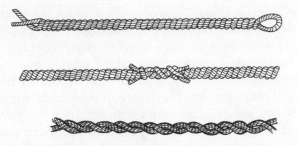

Top to bottom: (4) double the twisted leaf, allowing it to wind evenly around itself; (5) splice two doubled sections together; (6) after splicing several doubled sections together, twist the two strand rope again until you can double it once more, as in (4).

gether. To do that, untwist four or five turns from the free end of one length and pass each of the two strands through the doubled (loop) end of a second length from opposite sides. With that done, pull open the next twist beyond the doubled end and again thread the free ends through from opposite directions. Continue this process until you've threaded as much of the free ends of the first section into the twists of the second section as possible. A strong splice will require intertwining the free ends of one section through at least four of the twists of the second section.

After splicing together five or six three-foot sections, you're ready to double them again to make a stout four-strand rope. The easiest way I've found to do that is to bend the spliced lengths around a stake or cut-off tree branch and then twist each half even tighter in the same direction as its existing twist. You'll note that this means twisting one half clockwise and the other counterclockwise. I recommend holding one of the ends between your teeth as you turn the other. When the first half is twisted tight, reverse the ends, holding the end you've already twisted tight between your teeth as you apply torque to the second half. Once both halves of the bent cord have been twisted tightly enough to coil around themselves when the tension on them is released, hold the ends firmly together and allow them to wrap evenly around one another. Slide the doubled end off the stake, splice the free ends together to prevent them from unraveling, and you have a stout length of four-ply rope, although I think it's best to let the fibers dry for a day or two before use. And if you need a longer piece of rope, simply splice several four-strand sections together.

Again, handmade rope is inferior to its manufactured counterparts in terms of strength and durability. Exposed to the elements, it will rot to the point of uselessness within six months, but it is simple and quick to make with minimal practice, and it will serve well enough for many routine jobs. Note too that the same twist-lock method described here for making rope from plant fibers can be employed to turn string, or even thread, into very strong cord or rope. Even if you never need to use it, rope making is one skill that every serious woodsman should have in his inventory.

EMERGENCY HAMMOCK FISHING NET

One of the niftiest inventions to come along in recent years is the nylon mesh hammock. Made from super-strong twisted nylon string, the mesh hammock is lightweight and compact enough to fit in a jacket pocket, yet strong enough to support 500 pounds without breaking. I carry one in my backpack year-round because it provides me a fairly comfortable bed or seat in most any wooded terrain, no matter how swampy or frozen.

But the mesh hammock has a host of other uses as well. The hammock ghillie suit (see page 108) is just one of them. In an emergency survival situation, you can also use the mesh hammock—which already resembles a fishing net—to catch fish in almost any unfrozen stream or lake. I must point out, however, that the fishing techniques I'm about to describe are, like many emergency survival hunting methods, too efficient to be legal in most places. Every government in North America recognizes an individual's legal right to feed himself under conditions of starvation, but using these techniques to harvest fish otherwise—*in any scenario other than an emergency*—could result in a hefty fine.

Having said that, I'll begin by describing how to use the mesh hammock as a gill net. For those unfamiliar with the workings of this ancient fishing tool, a gill net consists of a wide mesh net suspended vertically in the water by floats fastened along one side (the top) and weights strung along the opposite (bottom) side. Schooling fish tend not to recognize the danger posed by this floating veil and will attempt to swim through it. Fish whose bodies are smaller than the mesh is wide will usually succeed, but if the fish is large enough to be obstructed by its pectoral or dorsal fins, or its own girth, it will likely attempt to back out of the net with quick thrashing motions. The result is that one or both of its gill covers will become caught on individual strings, making it impossible for the fish to pass through the net in either direction; its struggles usually result only in further entanglement. Few fish can escape from this trap without killing themselves in the process.

Because the mesh hammock already bears a strong resemblance to a commercial gill net, converting it is easy. Begin by spreading the hammock over the ground and fastening floats every six to eight inches along the length of one side. Floats should be made from dry, dead branches about two inches in diameter and cut or broken into lengths of no more than six inches. Cutting a shallow groove partway around the diameter of each float will prevent a string tied around it with a slipknot from sliding off. When tying the float strings to the hammock edge, take care to tie each one the same length to ensure the gill net will float evenly on the water.

The next step is to attach weights to the opposite edge of the hammock, which is now the bottom of your gill net. The easiest and fastest way I've found to do this is to crimp a large split-shot sinker about every four inches along the entire length of the hammock edge. If split-shot sinkers aren't available, stones can be substituted by laying them on top of a small piece of plastic sheeting, cloth, or mosquito netting and folding the sides up around the stone to form a bag. A slipknot tied with string around the bag's mouth will hold the stone securely in place when the string is tied to the hammock edge. Again, try to keep the strings, which should be kept as short as possible, in equal lengths.

With the hammock rigged, you're ready to catch fish. If the waterway to be fished is a stream or small river, the ends of the hammock should be tied off to each bank to keep it spread across the stream against the current. Ideally, the waterway should be as deep as the hammock is wide so that the net covers as much of it as possible, but the net will also work in shallower or deeper water.

The most productive time to fish a stream is of course during a spawning run, when certain species of fish swim upstream

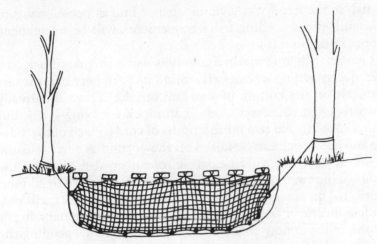

Add wooden floats and weights to an ordinary mesh hammock and stretch it across a stream to create an emergency gill net.

from adjacent lakes to mate. During these runs a net spread across the stream may, in a matter of minutes, catch more fish than you can use (unneeded fish can usually be released unharmed by gently disengaging them from the net by hand). At other times of the year it may be necessary to leave the net in place for a full day or more just to catch enough fish to eat. Wading up or down the stream toward the net while thrashing the water with a long pole often helps to drive fish into the net.

If the body of water you're fishing is a lake or pond with no current, it's best to spread the net in the water with only one end anchored to the shore. Some large fish—bass, for example—tend to inhabit deep water during the heat of the day, but travel close to shore before dawn and after sunset in search of smaller fish to eat. Perch, which are well camouflaged from above and below, are likely to be found cruising for food at any time of the day or night. In an emergency scenario, you won't want to wait for food, but patience is the key to successful open-water gillnetting so you'll probably want to find something else to attend to while you're waiting, like preparing a shelter to sleep in during the night. You'll know when you have a fish in the net if you give the anchor line an occasional gentle pull; the struggling fish's movements will be telegraphed through the taut line.

Another fishing method involves using the hammock as a dip net by adding weights all around its periphery to let it rest directly on the bottom of a stream or lake. There are already two ropes at each end of the hammock for tying it off, but you'll need to add two more lengths of cord to each of the sides so the hammock can be raised off the bottom as a net. Tie one cord on each side to the existing rope nearest it, then tie the ends of the two cords together. Another, longer (10- to 20-foot) cord tied on at the point where all six cords intersect will provide a means of raising the net. I recommend placing a log or stone in the center of the hammock and then suspending the hammock from a horizontal branch when tying on the extra four cords to make sure the lengths are equal. When you raise the weighted hammock off the ground, its sides and ends should come up to form a mesh bag that will keep fish from flopping out. When lowered to the ground, the hammock should lie flat. Remove the weight from its center and spread the hammock over the bottom of the stream or lake you intend to fish. When a fish swims into position over the net, quickly pull in the longer cord to cause the sides and ends of the hammock to close around it like a bag. In some cases it may help to tie the drawing cord off to a long pole or hang it over a convenient branch so the net will rise straight up from the bottom when pulled in.

Each of the techniques described here will allow you to catch fish with your hammock, but, again, there are an endless number of variations on these techniques that make them even more effective under specific emergency conditions. The one drawback to using your hammock is that its wide mesh may be so large that the only fish available are small enough to swim through. For that reason, it's probably a good idea to include a small gill net as part of your regular emergency survival kit. Packable 4×12-foot nets are available by mail from Brigade Quartermasters of Kennesaw, Georgia, for $12.00, plus shipping.

EMERGENCY SNOWSHOES

MATERIALS NEEDED:

▼

Tree branches or saplings

▼

Parachute cord or light rope

Nearly 20 years ago I read an article in *Esquire* magazine about a young couple and their baby who became stranded by a blizzard in one of our national forests. That story was burned into my memory by the fact that both the mother and her infant died from hypothermia before rescuers found them. The husband, who endured the hell of watching them freeze to death, lost all his toes to frostbite. The article also noted that one of the rangers sent to find folks in their situation became stranded himself. Incredibly, none of these three adults had the foresight to throw a pair of snowshoes into their vehicle, and the ranger's attempt to improvise a pair from his truck's floor mats was predictably futile.

Incidents like that one are what inspire me to teach others the wilderness survival techniques I've learned. If those folks—or the many more who have found themselves in similar circumstances every single year—had just known how to fashion a pair of emergency snowshoes, one or all of them might have walked out to safety. Slogging through knee-deep snow is heartbreaking work that frequently kills a person through exhaustion and hypothermia (caused by sweating) long before he or she reaches civilization. Under such circumstances, knowing how to construct a pair of emergency snowshoes might very well save your life.

Fashioning a pair of emergency snowshoes in the woods requires just three things: branches or saplings cut from the surrounding trees, a sharp, sturdy knife, and several feet of parachute cord or light rope. The wood used to make the frames should be strong and springy, yet easy to work with a knife. My preference is cedar, but maple, hickory, and ash also work well. Avoid using pine, poplar, or aspen because these woods tend to break rather than bend, and a broken snowshoe frame will effectively strand you until you can make repairs.

To make an emergency snowshoe (both snowshoes are identical), cut five sections of wood, each about one and one-half inches in diameter. Two of the sections should be about three feet long, while the remaining three are each cut to one-foot lengths. Whittle a notch about one inch wide and half an inch deep into each end of one of the one-foot lengths, making sure that both notches are on the same side. Next, cut identical notches into each end of the three-foot lengths, except on one length the notches should be on opposite sides. The two remaining one-foot lengths will be notched and used later.

Next, assemble the frame. Begin by laying the front-end (one-foot length) crosswise on the ground with both notches facing up. Lay the two three-foot pieces on top of this crosspiece, notches down so that all notches face and interlock with one another. Lash these three pieces tightly together at the intersections with an X-shaped pattern of cord (see illustration), tying the cords off with tight square knots. Then squeeze the free ends of the longer pieces together, making the frame a long triangle, and fit the downward notch into the upward notch. Lash this intersection together the same way, with an X-shape of cord tied off with a square knot.

The last two one-foot sections are used to support the wearer's foot as he or she steps down on the surface of the snow. Like the front crosspiece, these are notched, mounted from the underside, and lashed into position, except in this case their position on the frame is determined by the wearer's foot size. To determine the correct location, lay the assembled frame on the ground and place your foot inside it. Position your toes so that the front crosspiece clears the front of your boot by at least two inches. This clearance is important because the front of the snowshoe will swivel upward as you raise each foot. Once you've established that clearance, notch the remaining two crosspieces and tie them side-by-side at a point on the frame where they'll be directly under the arch of your foot, beginning just ahead of your boot heel. For some folks, it might be easier to use a single crosspiece here, but double crosspieces are less likely to bruise the bottoms of your feet on long treks.

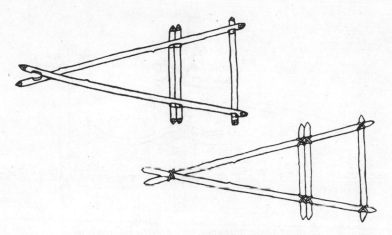

Make a functional emergency snowshoe by cutting and notching five saplings or branches (top), then lashing them together with rope or cord (bottom).

All that remains now is to fasten the snowshoes to your feet. The best way to do that is to lay the center of a three-foot length of paracord or rope across your instep, then run the ends under and around the arch crosspieces on each side of your foot. Bring both ends back up and cross them over your instep once again, then around your ankle joint, and tie them off at the front of your ankle. This method fastens the snowshoe securely to your foot while leaving your heel free to move up and down as the snowshoe swivels while you walk. The lacing should be tight, as it's sure to stretch to some degree during use.

With both snowshoes tied to your feet, take a short test walk to see how they work and to make any necessary adjustments. If you've never used snowshoes before you'll notice that they require a slightly straddled pace, with the feet wider apart than in the heel-toe walk that most of us are used to. When you raise your foot to take a step, the pointed tail of the shoe must be heavy enough to pull downward as the front end rises, swiveling on the arch crosspieces. If that doesn't happen, lash a heavy stick to the tail, make the frame longer, or move the arch crosspieces forward.

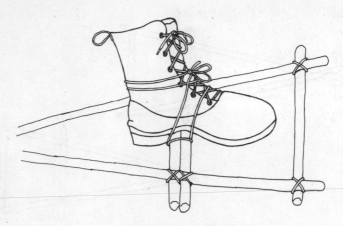

Lashing the emergency snowshoe to a pac boot.

Another problem you might encounter, especially if you're new to snowshoeing, is that of the binding cord sliding across the arch crosspieces, upsetting the balance of the snowshoe laterally. That problem is most easily remedied by cutting a small groove into the arch crosspieces on both sides of your foot to hold the bindings in place.

In actual use, you'll notice that these field-expedient snowshoes sink a bit deeper into the snow than commercial snowshoes, particularly in soft powder. That's because they don't have as much surface area as commercial snowshoes with leather lacing. Nonetheless, they do provide considerably more support in deep snow than boots alone, especially if the snow you're crossing is crusted with a layer of ice that won't quite hold your weight—conditions that often make each step a bone-jarring experience. In other words, the harder the snow is to walk through, the better the snowshoes will support you.

But under any conditions these snowshoes will function well enough to keep you from being stranded by heavy snow. Sinking a mere eight inches in waist-deep powder makes foot travel far less exhausting than it would be if you sank to your crotch with each step. Like the bow and drill firestarter (see page 208), you may never need to make a pair of emergency snowshoes, but if you ever do, knowing how could literally save your life.

SNARE TRIGGERS

The most difficult part of setting a spring snare for the purpose of capturing animals for food in an emergency survival situation is getting the trigger just right. Most triggers are by necessity made from wood, which is affected by changes in humidity and temperature. And since any snare is a more or less iffy proposition even under ideal conditions, anything you can do to make it more reliable will pay off.

The principle behind the trigger of any spring snare is to simply restrain or store up a force that will be sufficient to kill its intended prey with a device (a trigger) that will release that force as easily and quickly as possible. Ideally, the trigger will require only a minute amount of pressure from just one direction to separate, releasing the spring from its anchor point to apply its pent-up force to the prey. If the trigger requires too much pressure to separate, the prey might spook and evade the trap. And if the trigger is too sensitive, you'll find the snare tripping by itself every time a slight breeze touches it.

A number of reliable snare triggers can be fashioned in the field, or made at home and carried in the backpack. The most basic of these is the "bow knot trigger," so called because it uses a simple bow knot, just like the one we use to tie our shoelaces. In this case, however, one "shoelace" (usually nylon cord) is anchored in place by tying it around a stake driven into the ground, while the other is attached to the spring, usually a bent green sapling or branch. With the spring held in the bent position under pressure, tie a bow knot with the anchor and spring cords, just as if they were the two ends of a shoelace.

Once the spring has been secured to the anchor via the bow knot, all that remains is to set the tripping device. In most cases, that will be a snare loop which employs a sliding slipknot to ensnare an animal. Make sure the free end of the bow knot tied to the snare loop is attached to the spring, and not the anchor. When an animal passes through the noose and the noose begins to tighten, a pulling force will be exerted against

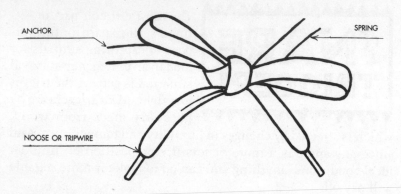

The bow knot snare trigger.

the free end of the bow knot, pulling the bow loop formed by it through the knot and causing the two cords to separate, releasing the spring, which in turn yanks hard against the snare loop. As you might have already guessed, decreasing the size of the bow loop formed by the spring cord also decreases the amount of pull required to release the snare, making the snare faster and more reliable.

Another good trigger made from cord is one I call the "loop trigger," because it uses three loops and a stick to hold the spring, anchor, and snare loop together. In this instance, first tie the ends of an eight-inch length (variable) of cord together with a square knot, forming a closed circle. Next, tie the free end of the anchor cord around the middle of that circle using a slipknot, resulting in two loops on either side of the anchor cord. Tie a third, nontightening loop of about the same diameter as those on the anchor cord in the end of the spring cord with a bowline knot or doubled overhand knot (see illustration). The snare noose is then tied off to the spring and situated so that the animal's head will be through it when the trigger is sprung.

To secure the spring and anchor cords together, bend the spring down until the three loops on their ends can be made to meet. Place the two loops of the anchor cord on each side of the loop in the end of the spring cord and insert a smooth stick through all three. The stick will serve, via the three loops, to

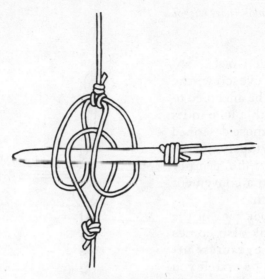

The loop snare trigger.

hold the two cords captive, and it also serves as the trigger release. Tying one side of a noose or a separate tripline onto the stick will give it the means to pull free when a pull is exerted against either.

Probably the fastest, lightest, and least expensive ready-made snare trigger I've found is the latch-hook trigger, made from the same latch-hook we've all used to secure screen doors and hinged windows. These can usually be purchased for less than one dollar from hardware and department stores, and they lend themselves very well to the business of snaring game. I recommend carrying a half dozen or so in your wilderness kit.

The beauty of the latch-hook trigger is that it can be used as is. The eyescrew through which the hook passes can be screwed directly into a convenient tree trunk or root from almost any direction to serve as both anchor and half of the trigger, although I generally prefer to substitute an eyescrew with a longer shank when I'm seeking larger game. Even the shank of the hook itself can be passed through the eye of the anchor screw to form a T-handle that provides extra torque for screwing into hardwoods. And in the unlikely event that you can find

The latch-hook snare trigger.

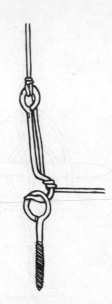

no suitable wood to an-
chor the eyescrew, the
hook can be anchored to
a cord with a loop in its
end, like those described
here previously, or the
hook can be simply
latched to a convenient
tree branch.

The hook part of the
latch-hook also comes
with an eyescrew at-
tached to its end. If you
plan to tie the hook di-
rectly onto the spring cord (my own preference), this eyescrew
must be removed at home before the trigger can be used because you'll need the eye on the end of the hook to tie off the
spring cord. But if you prefer to use the hook portion as the anchor, then of course the eye hook is left attached. Either way
will work, but I think the trigger is more reliable with the hook
tied to the spring cord.

The real beauty of the latch-hook trigger is that it can be
fine-tuned to catch anything from a squirrel to a deer. Filing a
small flat spot on the hook's inside bearing surface—the portion that makes contact with the anchor eyescrew—will allow
the trigger to be set for extreme sensitivity, while at the same
time making it stable enough not to trip from other outside in-
fluences. Under conditions of freezing rain or wet snow that
might cause other types of triggers to freeze up, a light film of
petroleum jelly or vegetable oil, both of which are essentially
scent-free, will keep the trigger at the sensitivity for which you
originally set it. Silicone spray also works well, although I sus-
pect animals can smell it.

Each of the triggers described thus far is easy to make and
very reliable if set correctly, and if you're snaring, having a good

trigger is at least half the battle. But a spring snare is made up of several components and it behooves you to know at least something about each of them. For instance, the spring is best made from bent saplings that are by their nature very springy, such as cedar, ash, or hickory. If possible, the amount of spring force restrained by the trigger and anchor should always be sufficient to raise the intended prey off the ground, guaranteeing a swift, humane kill with no possibility of escape. Likewise, the cord used should have a load rating of twice the animal's weight, yet it also needs to be as pliable and small in diameter as possible to make it more concealable. Whenever feasible, the snare noose is best made from wire twisted and tied onto the trigger cord because wire can literally cut through flesh, again resulting in a quick kill. Fencing wire is an excellent choice for deer, but for smaller animals like rabbits, fishing leader or picture-hanging wire works best.

As far as actually deploying the snare, that too is worthy of volumes. There are far too many variations to cover here, so I've provided illustrations to give you an idea how a basic spring snare should look when set. In most cases, the noose itself acts as the tripline, but if circumstances dictate that a separate tripline be used, remember that its opposite end will be anchored. It always pays to practice setting snares before you run into a situation where you might have to rely on your traps for food.

MAKING AND USING THE BOW AND DRILL

When our forebears settled this country they were, by today's standards, poorly equipped, not because they were trying to live up to some nonsensical macho image, but because they had no choice. They did, however, take full advantage of their then state-of-the-art flintlock rifles and forged iron blades because it would have been foolish—and even suicidal—not to. Today's outdoorsman would be well advised to follow those precedents and include as many modern conveniences in his or her pack as possible.

On the other hand, there's also a lot to be said for knowing how to perform some tasks the old way, before technology made them simple. None of us have much need to learn how to tan hides and sew them into garments with sinew and needles made from bone (why not just pack a sewing kit with steel needles?), but learning to build a fire using the bow and drill can be challenging and fun. It also adds one more skill to the woodsman's inventory, a skill that may stand him or her in good stead one day.

The principle behind the bow and drill fire-starting method is simple: A straight, dry softwood spindle (the drill) is rotated back and forth in the shallow hole of a flat, dry softwood fireboard. The hole is set close to the edge of the fireboard and has a notch in its outer perimeter to allow hot wood powder to overflow onto tinder material. The bowstring is wrapped once around the drill and, like a pulley, rotates the drill when the bow is drawn back and forth. A handle with a recessed hole to accommodate the top end of the drill and hold it securely as it spins is used to apply a light downward pressure, increasing the amount of heat and friction generated against the fireboard. The spinning action and downward pressure cause the fireboard and the bottom of the drill to become hot, creating a residue of blackened wood powder or "char." As the spinning and downward pressure continue, this powder will begin to smolder. The smoldering char continues to build up, falling through the notch in the fireboard hole and onto the combustible tinder, causing this to smolder as well. At this point the smoking tinder can be coaxed into flames by gently blowing against the live coals in its midst. Once the tinder has burst into flames, all that remains is to add wood, beginning with the smallest twigs and adding increasingly larger pieces as the fire grows stronger and hotter.

That's it in a nutshell. The principle is simple, but the actual construction and use of a bow and drill will require a bit more than knowing how it works. Native Americans, who relied heavily on this method of fire making before the introduction of flint and steel, matches, and finally butane lighters, had the use of the bow and drill down to an art. As with much of ancient Native American culture, many of the tips and tricks they learned to employ during lifetimes of experiences have been lost to the passage of time. But then, that's the very thing that makes learning to use the bow and drill so much fun: it's challenging to try to capture even a small part of an ancient culture. Every fire built by the bow and drill has within its flames the spirit of a people who centuries ago managed this land with a skill that the white man is only now beginning to understand.

Let's begin with the drill. Pine, poplar, cedar, aspen, and cottonwood are all good choices for a drill. Beech, maple, oak, locust, and birch are too dense to generate the all-important char in any quantity, although they too can be used if you are willing to invest time, muscle, and sweat. The ideal drill is made from the softest wood available. It must be completely dry, straight, and cleaned of bark. It should also be as round as possible. Based on my own experience, the ideal diameter is between one and two inches. A diameter of less than one inch won't provide the surface area necessary for the string to maintain good traction as it spins the drill, and a diameter of greater than two inches will create too much friction between the drill and handle, which will cause it to bind during use.

Drill length is also a consideration. The longer the drill, the harder it will be to hold steady during rotation. Too short a drill, however, will force the operator to work from a hunched position that can be very tiring, especially for those of us who are starting to feel the effects of age. The best drill length I've found is between 10 and 12 inches.

When you've selected a suitable drill, whittle one end to a sharp point beginning about two inches from the end. It's essential that you remove an equal amount of wood on all sides to keep the point in the center of the drill: in use, the drill will wobble to the same degree that the point is off-center. The point is the end of the drill that goes into the fireboard hole. The opposite end of the drill fits into the handle and you can simply round it off using a small knife or a rough stone.

The handle is made from a piece of wood roughly two and one-half inches wide by four inches long by two inches thick. These dimensions are for reference; try them first and then determine if a smaller or larger handle would better suit you.

The wood you select for the handle should be dry, and as hard as possible. The handle is used only to hold the drill steady during use and to allow you to exert slight downward pressure. The handle need not and should not get hot from friction. A dried hardwood such as maple or beech is best for making the handle, but poplar or pine will also work well.

The last step in making the handle is to drill a hole in the center of its bottom side. The hole should be about one inch deep and wide enough to loosely accommodate the blunt end of the drill. This operation can be accomplished by using the point of a hunting knife. You can create a custom fit between the drill and handle by dropping a little sand into the handle hole and forcefully rotating the blunt end of the drill inside it.

The fireboard is made from dry softwood. It should be no less than 18 inches long, at least 2 inches thick, and about 8 inches wide. It isn't essential that the fireboard be perfectly flat, but it should remain steady against the ground without wobbling during use.

Using your knife tip as an auger, gouge a hole in the right top corner of the fireboard to accommodate the pointed end of the drill. The depth of the finished hole should be about one inch and the diameter at the top of the hole should be approximately three-quarters the diameter of the drill. It's preferable to taper

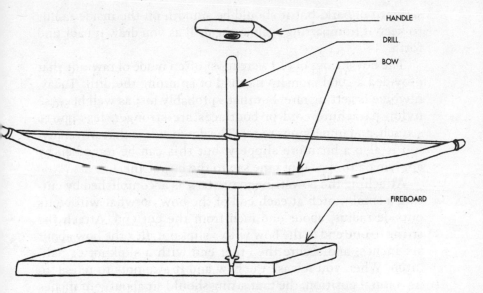

HANDLE

DRILL

BOW

FIREBOARD

Components of the bow and drill firestarter.

the hole toward the bottom. The outside edge of the hole should be no more than half an inch from the outer edge of the fireboard and no less than a quarter inch.

Next, cut a notch into the wall separating the edge of the hole from the outside edge of the fireboard. It's through this notch that the smoldering char will fall onto the tinder. The notch should extend to the bottom of the hole and be from one-half inch to three-quarters of an inch wide. The bottom of the notch should taper downward to further ensure that the char falls onto the tinder. A sawtooth-backed survival knife is ideal for fashioning the notch.

Next comes the bow. This is the least complicated part of the entire uncomplicated apparatus. In my experience, the ideal bow is one made from green river willow, cedar, red-osier dogwood, or any other springy green wood. The best candidate for a bow would be a sapling or branch about one inch in diameter and about three feet long. The bow need not flex more than six inches and should be sturdy enough to keep from flexing during use. It doesn't need to be perfectly straight or even stripped of bark, but it should be smooth on the inside radius to keep it from jarring against the drill as you draw it back and forth.

The bowstrings of old were most often made of rawhide that provided a good, nonslip method of spinning the drill. Today, rawhide is getting rare, but that's probably just as well because nylon parachute cord or bootlaces are stronger, less apt to stretch, and impervious to rot. The down side is that woven nylon is also a bit more slippery, but this can be remedied by applying a thin coat of pine sap to the bowstring.

Attaching the bowstring to the bow is accomplished by cutting a small notch at each end of the bow on what will be its outside radius, about one inch from the cut end. Attach the string to one end of the bow with a slipknot, flex the bow about six inches, and secure the other end with a slipknot or half-hitch. When you release the bow and it attempts to return to its natural position, the taut string should sit about four inches from the center of the bow.

Those are the four components of the bow and drill. The next step is to put them together so they can be used to build a fire. First, wrap the bowstring once around the drill with the drill inside between the string and the bow itself (see illustration). Next, fit the pointed end of the drill into the fireboard hole and the blunt end inside the hole in the handle. With your left hand, hold the drill vertical with the handle; grasp the near end of the bow with your right hand; and hold the fireboard steady by placing your left foot on it while kneeling on your right knee. With the bow held at the horizontal, begin moving it back and forth with long, smooth strokes while maintaining a firm but light downward pressure on the handle. Resting your left elbow on your upright left knee will help to keep the drill steady as it rotates inside the looped bowstring.

The idea is to create as much friction-induced heat at the fireboard end of the drill as possible. But without lubrication of some sort, the handle end of the drill will drag and is likely to become as hot as the fireboard end. Many survival instructors suggest that animal fat is a good lubricant in the field, but animal fat is often difficult to find and not worth the trouble. My own solution is to lubricate the hole in the handle with melted paraffin from an emergency candle. As the top of the drill heats up it melts the paraffin, making it slippery and liquid enough to be absorbed into the wood. Before long both the handle hole and the top of the drill have become hard, polished surfaces that mate perfectly and turn easily against one another with very little friction.

Starting a fire with the bow and drill will be a lot of work at first, so I suggest that the beginner practice back home, without tinder, until he or she can hold the component parts steady and get a good plume of smoke to rise from the fireboard hole. Adding a bit of sand in the fireboard hole will help increase the amount of friction generated by the spinning drill.

When you have achieved the expertise necessary to hold the handle and drill steady while sawing the bow back and forth, and are able to generate a steady stream of smoke from the fireboard, it's time to build a fire. A small pile of dry, easily combustible tinder is at least as important as any of the other components of the bow and drill. Cotton balls, cattail fluff, crushed blades of dried grass, powdered dry leaves, crushed dry reindeer moss, and even frayed cotton fabric have all been used successfully as tinder material. The only requirements are that the tinder be fibrous and that it ignite easily. I recommend a small supply of cotton balls in a Ziploc sandwich bag for the beginner. Cotton balls are perhaps the most flammable of tinder and are also both lightweight and inexpensive.

This is where the notch connecting the fireboard hole to its outside edge comes into play. Place a handful of well-frayed fibrous tinder on the ground next to the notch. Trapping a small portion of the tinder pile under the edge of the fireboard helps to hold it in place while you work the bow. As the drill begins to smoke, a hot, powdered char will begin to accumulate around its circumference. Continue working the bow and drill until the char overflows through the fireboard notch and onto the tinder pile. At this point you're nearly there. A few more strokes of the bow will cause the char to smolder, which in turn causes the tinder to smolder.

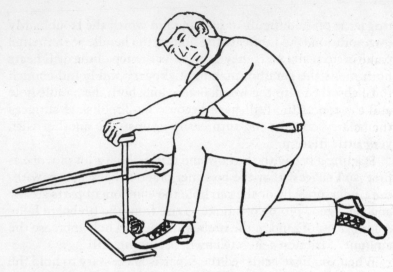

Using the bow and drill to start a fire.

When the tinder pile begins to smoke steadily, set the bow, drill, and handle aside and very gently slide the tinder pile into a cupped hand. Raise the smoldering tinder within a few inches of your mouth and blow into it with light, steady breaths through pursed lips. Forceful short breaths may extinguish the spark you've worked so hard to ignite, so blow as lightly and long as possible. Your efforts will be rewarded when the tinder suddenly bursts into flame. Drop the flaming tinder immediately into your prepared firepit—that goes without saying—and add more tinder to keep the flames alive. Position small, dry twigs tepee-fashion around the burning tinder and as soon as they begin to catch fire, add progressively larger sticks until the fire is the desired size.

On paper, using the bow and drill to start a fire sounds easy. It really isn't, especially for beginners. At first, the arm working the bow will no doubt become fatigued quickly and those of us who can no longer remember our 30th birthdays may feel the strain on back muscles and joints. But is making and using the bow and drill worth the effort required to attain proficiency? You bet it is. The average beginner will spend between 20 and 30 minutes working the tool before succeeding in getting a fire started, but all the sweat and effort will be instantly forgotten with the first flames. Fatigue will disappear in the wake of exhilaration, satisfaction, and a certain sense of magic as the fire builder feels drawn back to a time when human survival was subject to the whims of nature and only the ability to make fire separated humans from the animals. A fire built with the bow and drill is a thing of value, something to be appreciated and carefully tended.

Romance notwithstanding, I will continue to start the majority of my own campfires with modern tools simply because they're abundantly available, faster to use, and a lot less work. The bow and drill is challenging, and I firmly believe that all of us who are serious about camping or any other wilderness activity owe it to ourselves to become familiar with its construction and use, but its real utility is as an emergency survival tool. Can any of us ever have too many survival skills?